TESTIMONIALS

"The Massachusetts Biotech Boom: Keeping Your Wealth Intact is a must-read for anyone working in the life sciences industry or considering entering it. Kevin O'Brien acclimates the reader to a solid, top-down history of the Massachusetts life sciences eco-system, while illuminating the opportunities, as well as the risks, that exist today. A great tool to navigate an entrepreneurial or executive career track in one of the most dynamic industries today!"

—Christopher Coghlin

President and CEO, Coghlin Companies, Cogmedix, ColumbiaTech

"The Massachusetts Biotech Boom articulates how the need for long-term perspective, perseverance, and an appetite for financial risk has been a critical ingredient of new emerging products and companies ... It's also a wonderful read for individuals seeking a career in this field and for those currently employed in the industry; it is a great aid for harnessing the knowledge contained within to become more financially successful."

—Abraham W. Haddad, DMD, FAAHD

Chairman, Massachusetts Biomedical Initiatives

"*Through this book,* The Massachusetts Biotech Boom: Keeping Your Wealth Intact, *readers will gain clarity and knowledge of the BioTech industry and landscape, which can enable them to broaden and enhance their careers within it. In addition, they will obtain an understanding of the most current and advanced wealth management strategies employed by successful executives and entrepreneurs available through the tax code today.*"

—Richard C. Barry, Esq.

Estate and business planning attorney

"The Massachusetts Biotech Boom *has practical insights and is a useful resource for biotech executives and key employees seeking financial planning guidance on a range of issues including equity compensation.*"

—Bruce Brumberg

Editor and cofounder, myStockOptions.com; myNQDC.com

THE MASSACHUSETTS
BIOTECH
BOOM

A Guide for

EXECUTIVES & ENTREPRENEURS

THE MASSACHUSETTS

BIOTECH
BOOM

KEEPING YOUR WEALTH INTACT

KEVIN M. O'BRIEN
CFP™, AIF™, CAP™

Published by Advantage, Charleston, South Carolina.
Member of Advantage Media Group.

ADVANTAGE is a registered trademark, and the Advantage colophon is a trademark of Advantage Media Group, Inc.

Printed in the United States of America.

10 9 8 7 6 5 4 3 2 1

ISBN: 978-1-59932-880-5
LCCN: 2019932445

Cover design by George Stevens.
Layout design by Melanie Cloth.

This publication is designed to provide accurate and authoritative information in regard to the subject matter covered. It is sold with the understanding that the publisher is not engaged in rendering legal, accounting, or other professional services. If legal advice or other expert assistance is required, the services of a competent professional person should be sought.

Advantage Media Group is proud to be a part of the Tree Neutral® program. Tree Neutral offsets the number of trees consumed in the production and printing of this book by taking proactive steps such as planting trees in direct proportion to the number of trees used to print books. To learn more about Tree Neutral, please visit **www.treeneutral.com**.

Advantage Media Group is a publisher of business, self-improvement, and professional development books and online learning. We help entrepreneurs, business leaders, and professionals share their Stories, Passion, and Knowledge to help others Learn & Grow. Do you have a manuscript or book idea that you would like us to consider for publishing? Please visit **advantagefamily.com** or call **1.866.775.1696**.

This book is dedicated to you! The entrepreneurs, business owners, and employees in the life sciences and other industries who achieve greatness every day and who don't always receive the recognition for doing so. My hope is that you gain clarity and purpose from reading this book, and that it helps you to achieve your professional purpose and life goals.

To the past and present members of the CFP board: Your undying commitment to a uniform standard of competence and ethics is invaluable to the sustainability of our profession.

TABLE OF CONTENTS

SECTION I

THE BOOM!

SECTION II

FOR ENTREPRENEURS

SECTION III

FOR EXECUTIVES AND UPPER MANAGEMENT

ACKNOWLEDGMENTS

As you know, just like yourself, something like this cannot be done alone. This book wouldn't have been possible or worthwhile without the loving support of my wife, Ree, and my adult children, Kilian and Fallon.

This book was inspired by my work with the founders, coaches, and members of CEG Worldwide and CEG Advantage. Thank you.

I sincerely thank Dr. Abraham "Abe" Haddad, chair of the Massachusetts Biomedical Initiatives, for his enthusiasm, guidance, friendship, and honest critiquing throughout the journey.

Many people gave of their time and knowledge throughout the interviewing process, especially 1980 Nobel Prize winner Walter "Wally" Gilbert. I am humbled and amazed by your commitment to a field of study and commercialization that has such an incredible impact on humanity.

I thank Kevin Gillis, Bill Duke, and Jonathan Freve—all CFOs—for enlightening me on the details, challenges, and victories along the path of startup, funding, commercialization, and exit.

Dennis Guberski and David Easson's local, real-world experience of founding, running, and growing biotech companies allowed me to peer into "the trenches" and illuminated the risks and rewards of entrepreneurship in this remarkable industry.

Tom Andrews, co-president and regional market director for Alexandria Real Estate Equities, gave credence to how the "ripples" of the industry award ancillary businesses, creating a vast and diverse ecosystem.

ABOUT THE AUTHOR

Kevin M. O'Brien first entered the financial services industry in 1986 and, since then, as founder and president of Peak Financial Services, Inc., he has helped hundreds of individuals and organizations reach their financial goals. A popular speaker at many business, civic, and nonprofit organization events, he has published articles in local and national news media, including the *Worcester Business Journal, U.S. News & World Report, Investopedia,* and *TheStreet.com.* He also wrote the foreword to *The Art of Investing & Portfolio Management: A Proven 6-Step Process to Meet Your Financial Goals.* Kevin has served on the board of governors for Tufts Medical Center and Reliant Medical Group Foundation, and is past president of the Planned Giving Council of Central Massachusetts, where he led the organization in coordinating speaking events and educational formats for the nonprofit community. A longtime member of the International Financial Planning Association, he is a corporator for the Worcester Community Foundation and the YWCA of Worcester, Massachusetts. Kevin also volunteers his time on the finance committee of Worcester Country Club. Married to his soulmate, Ree, since 1989, he is the father of two wonderful adult children: Kilian, a graduate of Cornell's Hotel School, who serves in a management role with Hersha Hospitality Management; and Fallon, a senior at Shrewsbury High School and a competitive dancer with Elite Academy of Dance. When not at work, Kevin can be found at the gym, playing golf, or spending time with his family.

FOREWORD

by Abraham W. Haddad, DMD, FAAHD

The Massachusetts Biotech Boom is a highly relevant and timely book. It is compelling, informational, and right on point. As many of us have witnessed or read about, the Massachusetts biotech industry has grown exponentially over the past two decades, with innovation leading to tremendous success for some entrepreneurs while others realize major setbacks. For those companies that emerge into success stories, we have seen significant wealth accumulated by owners, shareholders, and employees with stock options and other equity incentive compensation plans. We have also witnessed a shift from large corporations to smaller and much more versatile business start-ups and incubators over the years, creating an environment for investors to become more engaged. *The Massachusetts Biotech Boom* articulates how the need for long-term perspective, perseverance, and an appetite for financial risk has been a critical ingredient of new emerging products and companies. In the area of biotechnology and life sciences today, particularly the timeline from concept to product launch, we have seen entrepreneurs taking much greater risks to get to market. This book is packed with interesting interviews from some of the most well respected entrepreneurs in the life sciences industry. Author Kevin O'Brien shares his perspectives and knowledge of the industry while weaving in the principles of how to harness wealth creation and preservation. While even successful biotech entities are at risk, O'Brien shares the challenges and uncertainties, and demonstrates the need for a roadmap.

The rationale discussed in each of the chapters leads to a logical and rational basis for decision making in the subjects covered. The conclusions and takeaways of the chapters are concise and allow the uninitiated in the matters of finance to reach relevant conclusions to their particular circumstances at various stages of their product and company developments. The historical review of the emergence of and challenges facing the field of biotechnology clearly allow the reader to have an awareness of the environmental, technical, and scientific circumstances that have brought us to where we are today.

This book is an excellent tool for those seeking to leverage their investments in biotechnology or life sciences, and a great guide to those new investors striving to understand the industry to deepen their portfolios. It's also a wonderful read for individuals seeking a career in this field and for those currently employed in the industry; it is a great aid for harnessing the knowledge contained within to become more financially successful.

SECTION I

THE BOOM!

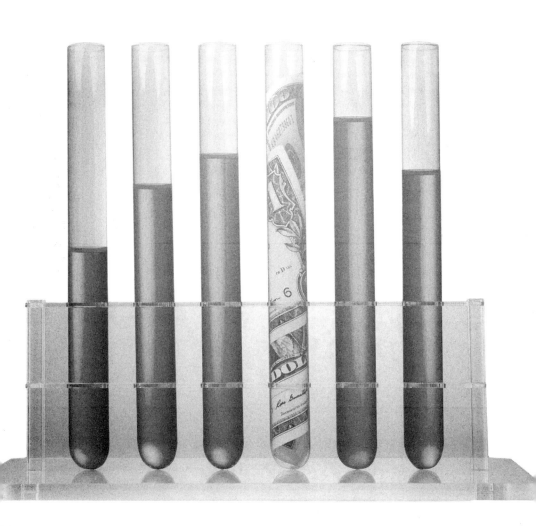

INTRODUCTION

THE BOOM
BEGINS

> Boom: A period of significant output within a population. The period is marked by productivity increases, sales increases, wage increases, and rising demand. An economic boom may be accompanied by a period of inflation.[1]

This definition fits both the birth and expansion of the biotechnology industry. However, that boom was not a one-time occurrence that took place and ended as suddenly as it began. Instead, it was any number of booms, some of which rose and kept rising, and some that fell, sometimes when they were barely off the ground. Success in the industry depends on how one can navigate these often rapidly occurring events.

The timeline reads like a fast-paced screenplay.

1976-77—Cambridge City Council holds hearings on the safety of recombinant DNA research and passes the country's first ordinance regulating the work.

1978—In Geneva, Switzerland, three venture capitalists and a group of scientists led by Harvard University professor and molecular biology pioneer Walter Gilbert, and MIT professor Phillip Sharp, establish Biogen, a pharmaceutical company with an emphasis on biological breakthroughs.

1980—Walter Gilbert wins the Nobel Prize in chemistry for his work in DNA sequencing.

1982—Biogen opens a new headquarters facility in Cambridge, Massachusetts, and becomes a NAS-

---

1   BusinessDictionary, s.v. "economic boom," accessed January 2019, http://www.businessdictionary.com/definition/economic-boom.html.

That was just the beginning, of course. Genzyme Corporation arrived in 1981, setting up business on the seventeenth floor of a building in Boston's Chinatown. In 1982, the Food and Drug Administration approved the first biotechnology therapy, a human insulin drug made by Genentech. That same year Whitehead Institute was founded in Cambridge. A leading research center, it provided approximately one-third of the human genome sequence in 2000.[2]

Now, thirty-five-plus years later, look where the industry has been, what we have accomplished, and where we are heading.

- Deloitte estimates that by 2020, 10.5 percent of global GDP will be spent on healthcare, with about $4 trillion spent on cardiovascular, cancer, and respiratory diseases.[3]

- In Massachusetts, industry jobs grew by 28 percent in the last ten years and by 4.3 percent in one year.[4]

- Massachusetts biotech R&D spending increased 35 percent since 2008.[5]

- At the end of 2017, Massachusetts biotech companies employed 69,941 workers with an average salary of $149,731, totaling more than $10.4 billion in wages.

---

2   "The History of Biotechnology," boston.com, http://archive.boston.com/business/specials/bio2007/timeline/.

3   Deloitte, "2017 Global Healthcare Outlook," https://www2.deloitte.com/content/dam/Deloitte/global/Documents/Life-Sciences-Health-Care/gx-lshc-2017-health-care-outlook-infographic.pdf.

4   Massachusetts Biotechnology Council, "2018 Industry Snapshot," accessed January 2019, http://files.massbio.org/file/MassBio-2018-Industry-Snapshot-FINAL-8-29-18.pdf.

5   Ibid.

- In the last ten years, 12 million square feet of commercial lab space has been added to Massachusetts, an increase of 71 percent. The boom hasn't let up.[6]

- Venture investment in Massachusetts biopharma companies was $3.1 billion in 2017, up from $2.9 billion in 2016, and more than triple the amount invested in 2012.

- Massachusetts has more employees classified as biotechnology R&D than any other state.[7]

- Finally, venture capitalists and angel investors aren't the only ones pouring money into Massachusetts biotech. The state received $2.7 billion of the National Institutes of Health budget in 2017, the highest per capita amount in the country.[8]

The spectrum of biotech goes from startup companies in need of money to big pharma firms with deep pockets. Between the two are companies of assorted sizes—some doing well, and others struggling. In addition, ancillary businesses, such as accounting, law, real estate, office supplies, and even coffee shops, are benefiting from the biotech ecosystem.

Opportunities and Risks

All this growth adds up to a booming industry that continues to expand and create wealth and investment opportunities along with products that change and even save lives. There's a multiplier effect

---

6   Ibid.
7   Ibid.
8   The Boston Planning & Development Agency Research Division, "Boston: Most NIH Funds for 23 Consecutive Years," February 2018, http://www.bostonplans.org/getattachment/5cac1d8e-6fd7-4931-a029-6e5f39a28947: 12.

as well. Investment by the government and venture capitalists multiplies three to five times throughout the economy. For executives and upper management within the biotech industry, the career opportunities are above average because the industry is surging, and startup companies are continuing to emerge.

As these companies transition from startup to maturity, they create a need for sales and marketing executives, supply chain management personnel, and accounting and finance staff. Thus, every faction of the workforce is affected positively.

That doesn't mean risk isn't prevalent in the biotech industry. If a drug doesn't pass FDA testing, a promising company can shut down overnight. Companies can be so certain of success that they'll be ready to celebrate with champagne in the boardroom, only to learn their drug has failed approval and they'll be out of business the next day. As with any high-risk, high-reward opportunity, navigating the biotechnology industry requires knowledge, experience, patience, and a little luck.

My hope is that this book will enhance your knowledge of the Massachusetts biotechnology industry and help you identify opportunities and mitigate risks as you navigate your career in this dynamic and life-changing industry—all while keeping your wealth intact!

My Background

I majored in finance and graduated from Merrimack College in 1985. Initially, I had planned on being a stockbroker, but as I gained more academic and life experience, I decided to pursue a career where I could to do more for my clients. In the mid-1970s I witnessed my father, who worked as an accountant for more than twenty-eight years at the same company, lose his job. Two years prior to his retirement, the company was bought and immediately liquidated. This happened before the ERISA laws, which protect employee retirement plans, were in place. The company was sold, and the retirement plan was eliminated. My father was never the same after that, and it left an indelible impact on me. I was determined to control my own destiny and to provide a service that would prevent others from experiencing financial disaster. Subsequently, I became a financial advisor, and now provide my clients with a five-step comprehensive wealth management process designed for them to enjoy, enhance, protect, and ultimately transfer their wealth efficiently and effectively.

I started my financial career at the beginning of the biotech boom, while the computer industry was in full swing. Companies like Digital Equipment Corp, Data General, and EMC were creating jobs and wealth, while the biotech industry was still fledgling. Many of our early clients were high-tech executives and high-level managers. Like our clients in the biotech industry today, many of these clients obtained their wealth through equity incentive compensation plans, like stock options, restricted stock, and deferred compensation plans. Through our wealth management process, we have successfully helped hundreds of these early clients provide a college education for their children, buy second homes, secure their retirement lifestyles, fulfill their charitable intent, and successfully transfer their wealth to the next generation. We continue to enjoy doing the same with participants in the biotech industry today.

What This Book Can Do for You

By documenting the general history, and celebrating the milestones and breakthroughs, of the Massachusetts biotechnology industry, the intent of this book is to motivate you to persist upon an entrepreneurial path or build upon a successful career within this industry. You'll identify the entrepreneurial and executive career opportunities within this space while understanding the risks that persist to this day. In the end, you'll learn how our comprehensive five-step wealth management process can help you mitigate the risks and allow you to move forward with clarity and direction, while building your career or creating businesses, with a successful exit in mind.

Kevin O'Brien, CFP®, AIF®, CAP®

CHAPTER ONE

THE BASE OF THE BOOM

Initially, the biotech boom was all about the science. Money would come later. The universities provided the initial infrastructure and impetus to kick-start Cambridge-Boston's biotech growth, then to land some key anchor companies, and, ultimately, to fuel the spread of the industry. In a way, what happened in Massachusetts was like the Old West, with biotechnology as the gold.

In the Beginning, Biogen

In the introduction, I mentioned Walter Gilbert, whom I interviewed while writing the book and conducting research for future articles. Born in 1932, Wally Gilbert, as he's known in the industry, was one of the early pioneers. In 1978, he and another eventual Nobel laureate, MIT professor Phillip Sharp, a co-discoverer of RNA splicing along with several other scientists, founded Biogen in Geneva, Switzerland. Gilbert won the Nobel Prize in 1980, and in 1982, the company opened a new facility in Cambridge, Massachusetts, and transferred its headquarters to that city. Gilbert would go on to co-found Paratek Pharmaceuticals, which he ran until 2014.

At the beginning, even with a highly reputed founding team at Biogen, the company struggled. Even today, struggling is a common fate for biotech startups, for four reasons: first, because of the difficult science involved; second, because of the need to pass FDA trials; third, because of the general difficulties of getting a startup off the ground; and finally, because most of these startups lack enough money.

Jim Vincent, who took over as Biogen CEO in 1985, is credited by many with turning the company into a profitable enterprise.

"Biogen's survival as a freestanding company was really a product of Jim's leadership and his business skills," Sharp told the *Boston Globe* for Vincent's 2013 obituary.[9]

Biogen merged with IDEC in 2002, becoming Biogen Idec—until 2015, when it reverted to its original name. Biogen has taken a position at the forefront of the fight against multiple sclerosis and is addressing some of the most challenging and complex diseases of the brain, including Alzheimer's and Parkinson's.

Genzyme: Multiple Sclerosis, HIV, and Rare Diseases

In 1981, Genzyme, another major biotech firm, was founded by Sheridan Snyder, George M. Whitesides, and Henry Blair, a technician at the New England Enzyme Center at Tufts Medical School. Their goal was to help patients with difficult-to-treat medical conditions.

As with Biogen, the key executive to turn Genzyme into a powerhouse came aboard after the earliest days. Henri Termeer was credited with building the company from a small research organization into a major corporation. The Netherlands-born Termeer was also considered one of the most influential leaders in biotech.

Ed Kaye, a former Genzyme employee who would go on to lead Sarepta Therapeutics, told the *Boston Business Journal* in a 2017 obituary for Termeer, "I think at last count over 55 CEOs of [biotech] companies were from Genzyme. He was the oracle of Marblehead ...

---

9   Bryan Marquard, "James L. Vincent, 73; helped turn biotech into a winner," December 16, 2013, https://www.bostonglobe.com/metro/obituaries/2013/12/16/james-vincent-weston-ceo-and-chairman-turned-around-biogen-fortunes/eof7YW42RkZvpHLfQtnmMO/story.html.

the idea that a CEO could be as generous with his time as he was, is unheard of."[10]

By 2010, Genzyme reported $4 billion in revenue and was the fourth-largest US biopharmaceutical company. The following year, Sanofi bought the company for $20.1 billion. Today, still owned by Sanofi, Genzyme is a leader in both the treatment of multiple sclerosis and rare diseases.

Vertex: Cystic Fibrosis and Hepatitis C

In 1989, Joshua Boger founded Vertex Pharmaceuticals in Cambridge. In a departure from other drug developers, the company used advanced computer programs to identify compounds for new drugs. Since its founding, Vertex has developed drugs to fight HIV, cystic fibrosis, and hepatitis C.

One of the largest parts of Vertex Pharmaceuticals's success story is its focus on helping people with cystic fibrosis, a focus that almost didn't happen. In 2001, Vertex had come out with its new HIV drug, and although the company wasn't profitable, it was not running out of cash.

Still, Boger decided to accept a $500,000 contract from the Cystic Fibrosis Foundation to try to develop drugs to treat that disease. Approximately thirty thousand people in the US are afflicted with cystic fibrosis, so such a drug was unlikely to make much money.[11] Yet cystic fibrosis is a life-shortening genetic disease. The

---

10   W. Mark Bernau, "Henri Termeer, 'Giant of Biotech' and Longtime CEO of Genzyme, Dies at 71," *Boston Business Journal,* May 13, 2017, " https://www.bizjournals.com/boston/news/2017/05/13/henri-termeer-giant-of-biotech-and-longtime-ceo-of.html.

11   Cystic Fibrosis Foundation, "2017 Patient Registry Annual Data Report," August 2018, https://www.cff.org/Research/Researcher-Resources/Patient-Registry/2017-Patient-Registry-Annual-Data-Report.pdf.

gene causing it was first cloned by NIH-supported academic scientists in 1989. Based upon this discovery, Vertex scientists started a research effort in the late 1990s to discover transformative therapies to treat the underlying causes of the disease.

Boger's team succeeded, rolling out Kalydeco, Vertex's first drug for the disease, in 2012, and its cystic fibrosis treatment has also become a significant contributor to the company's bottom line. By 2017, Vertex employed 2,100 people around the world, with two-thirds of those employees focused on research. The Weymouth, Massachusetts, location opened in 1995, and serves as the company's world headquarters. The Boston office opened in late 2009 because company principals wanted to be closer to some of Vertex's larger, longer-term environmental and construction projects.

Genzyme, Biogen, and Vertex are just three examples, although very prominent ones, of the path to success for Massachusetts biotech. As the name changes over time indicate, large pharmaceutical companies have been attracted to the state's biotech cluster. In 2002, Novartis from Great Britain and AstraZeneca from Switzerland came into the area. Illinois-based Baxter, whose highest-profile products include therapies to treat the blood-clotting disorder hemophilia, arrived in 2015 and agreed to a $32 billion takeover by Shire, an Irish pharmaceutical giant.

During the biotech boom's infancy in 1982, philanthropist Edwin C. "Jack" Whitehead and MIT professor and Nobel Laureate David Baltimore established the world-renowned Whitehead Institute for Biomedical Research in Cambridge.

Whitehead was driven by the vision of assembling a group of some of the world's best scientific researchers under one roof and eliminating obstacles to their pursuit of discovery. Baltimore helped forge a relationship between the Whitehead Institute and MIT and became the institute's founding director.

Whitehead made a fortune manufacturing laboratory equipment and saw his funding for biotech research as a way to give back. He initially donated $7.5 million, then another $35 million to build the institute, and he pledged $100 million annually to be paid out of a trust after his death, the New York Times reported in his 1992 obituary.[12]

"Jack was an extraordinary man who started with little, built an enormous fortune and then dedicated himself to using it in an imaginative and personal way that made a major contribution to biomedical research," Baltimore told the *Times*.[13]

Less than a decade after its founding, the Whitehead Institute was named the top research institution in the world for molecular biology and genetics. In 2000, it became the single largest contributor to the mapping of the human genome. Currently, the Whitehead Institute is mapping stem cell circuitry, investigating protein folding problems, probing newly discovered RNAs, and more. The institute continues to be a leader in the life sciences industry.

Discussions among the Whitehead Institute, MIT, Harvard and its affiliated hospitals, and philanthropists Eli and Edythe Broad, eventually led to the creation of the Broad Institute in 2004. The institute almost failed to materialize because of a rivalry between MIT and Harvard and because of concerns at Harvard-affiliated hospitals about cannibalizing research.

"My wife and I believe the most important thing we will have done in our lifetimes is to be involved in the creating of the Broad

---

12   Kathleen Teltsch, "Edwin C. Whitehead, 72, Dies; Financed Biomedical Research," *New York Times,* February 4, 1992, https://www.nytimes.com/1992/02/04/nyregion/edwin-c-whitehead-72-dies-financed-biomedical-research.html.

13   Ibid.

Institute," Eli Broad, founder of KB Homes, told the *New York Times* in 2012.[14]

The Broad Institute focuses on using genomics to further the understanding of disease and build a foundation for the development of genetic therapies. By 2017, the Broads had donated $600 million to back scientists' biomedical research.

The institute sees itself as a pioneer in scientific research because it combines disciplines such as biology, chemistry, computer science, and engineering to fuel its explorations.

By 2009, the Boston Consulting Group had named Kendall Square near MIT the "most innovative square mile on earth," for its dense population of biotech and information technology companies.[15]

Why Massachusetts?

Massachusetts was blessed with key advantages at the dawn of the biotech age in the 1970s and 1980s. The state was home to some of the greatest hospitals and universities in the world, including Harvard, MIT, and the University of Massachusetts. Many of the top researchers in the field did their finest work there. Hospitals such as Mass General were forging the future of medicine. Those institutions helped prime the pump for the biotech revolution. In those days, the research departments of institutions such as Harvard, MIT, and UMass Medical School began focusing on recombinant DNA research. This led to the Cambridge City Council holding hearings on the safety of this research in 1976 to 1977.

---

14   Stephanie Strom, "A Collaboration That Began with a Disastrous Lunch," *New York Times,* January 2, 2012, https://www.nytimes.com/2012/01/03/science/broad-institute-collaboration-began-with-a-disastrous-lunch.html.
15   Noel Rubinton, "Where to See (Really See) the Art of Maya Lin," October 20, 2017, https://www.nytimes.com/2017/10/20/travel/where-to-see-really-see-the-art-of-maya-lin.html.

Citizens and local politicians expressed concerns about the public safety and the National Institute of Health's ability to regulate and oversee these laboratory experiments. Until that occurred, no one knew the ultimate outcome. Subsequently, the council passed an ordinance that would regulate the work. Although that regulation was a response to research that was already happening, it also helped set the stage for Cambridge to become a center of the biotech boom that was just about to happen.

I recently asked Walter Gilbert whether he was targeting particular diseases that had affected friends or family members. "No," he said.

He continued, "That is often the reason people go into medical school. It's not a reason for doing the more abstract science. It's not generally the motivation. The most productive part of science is the basic research, and that is essentially curiosity driven. It's not driven to a particular disease. Applied research seems to be driven to a particular disease. That's what big pharma constantly does. You've already decided what diseases you are going to work on, and you work on those. We're willing to back any disease. If you have to make a breakthrough, you may have to discover something entirely novel in order to get there, but that novel thing may easily come out of some of other form of research that you don't expect."

Gilbert's answer sums up what motivates many in biotech: this is an industry driven by curiosity, and that curiosity often delivers great rewards.

Growth and More Growth

As the biotech industry grew, so did my own firm, Peak Financial Services. Manufacturing almost vanished from the state during the 1970s and 1980s, leaving the nearby city of Worcester, home of UMass Medical School, with sad and empty old mill buildings. I remember driving down I-290, the main interstate through the city, looking over at the center, and seeing a landscape crowded with boarded-up brick buildings. As the buildings aged, they became safety hazards.

But something unexpected and exciting happened amidst all that decay. Thanks to the life sciences, new life took root in Worcester and, of course, the entire state. Over the past thirty years, biotech and medical device design and manufacturing companies have risen to prominence, leading to an economic renaissance that began in Cambridge and Boston and spread to Worcester and other cities in the Bay State. Today, Worcester is home to more than fifty biotechnology companies and eighteen colleges, namely WPI and UMass Medical School, with curricula geared toward the industry.

When I drive down I-290 now, I see many of those vacant factories have been torn down, and new modern buildings have risen in their place. The Worcester area was named a Center of Excellence in Biotechnology in 1985 by Gov. Michael Dukakis. Four such technology centers in the state focus on integrating state universities into local economies. The presence of the University of Massachusetts Medical School made Worcester a natural choice as a biotech hub.

In 1985, the Massachusetts Biotechnology Research Park was created near Worcester. The governor's office played a major hand in recruiting companies to the new facility. With almost one million square feet of building space and 105 acres, the park continues to grow, has become a leading center of biotech research and production, and is home to more than a dozen biotech companies.

But the biotech revolution in Massachusetts has been about more than clearing away eyesores and replacing them with gleaming new buildings. It has been a tremendous generator of new companies, jobs, hope, and wealth. The life sciences have also replaced stagnant business models with dynamic new ones.

As the years have gone by, the clusters in Worcester and Cambridge-Boston have grown together. The president of the Cambridge-based Massachusetts Biotechnology Council (MassBio) sits on the board of trustees of the Massachusetts Biomedical Initiative, based in Worcester, and bolstering the public transportation system continues. This all amounts to a history that has resulted in a dynamic new economic driver for Massachusetts, which includes therapeutics, medical devices, R&D-type companies that sell equipment for academic research and development, and the whole healthcare industry as an end user.

On January 6, 2017, Governor Charlie Baker signed legislation authorizing the transfer of forty-four acres of land to the Worcester Business Development Corporation for the creation of the Worcester Biomanufacturing Park under the Baker/Polito Administration's "Open for Business" initiative. The forty-four-acre park adds five hundred thousand square feet of biomanufacturing capacity within the City of Worcester. WuXi Biologics of China recently announced it will build a $60 million biomanufacturing facility at the new Worcester Biomanufacturing Park, which will create one hundred and fifty new jobs locally.

"Many partners of WuXi are within two hours of the new site. We are all very excited to initiate our first U.S. site to enable local companies and expedite biologics development in the U.S.," said Dr. Chris Chen, CEO of WuXi.[16]

---

16   Zachary Comeau, "Chinese company to build $60M biomanufacturing facility in Worcester," June 11, 2018, http://www.wbjournal.com/article/20180611/NEWS01/180619998/ chinese-company-to-build-60m-biomanufacturing-facility-in-worcester.

The expansion of the biotech industry in this state is creating plenty of wealth, and, as always, that wealth comes with commensurate risk. My colleagues and I at Peak Financial Services are well-equipped and positioned to guide executives and entrepreneurs in planning for the future. In a field like biotech, which has become enormously important to our region, that planning is crucial, as you will see throughout this book. We will explore the growth of the biotech industry in Massachusetts, the ecosystem as it stands today, the costs and benefits of working in such a high-risk, high-reward industry, and how you can plan to maximize those benefits while mitigating the risks.

"We are in a new era of medicine where breakthrough science and personalized therapies are transforming the way we treat patients. Robust investment in research and development by biopharmaceutical companies has resulted in advances and discoveries unlike anything we've seen before. In the last decade we have invested half a trillion dollars and these investments are just beginning to pay off."[17]

Now that we've looked at the foundation of the biotech boom, in chapter 2 let's see where it is today.

---

17   PhRMA, "2018 Profile Biopharmaceutical Research Industry," accessed January 2019, http://phrma-docs.phrma.org/industryprofile/2018/pdfs/2018_IndustryProfile_Brochure.pdf.

Takeaway

- Universities provided the initial infrastructure and impetus to fuel growth of the biotech industry in Cambridge-Boston.

- Genzyme, Biogen, and Vertex are just three examples, although very prominent ones, of the path to success for Massachusetts biotech.

- Massachusetts was blessed with key advantages at the dawn of the biotech age. The state is home to some of the greatest hospitals and universities in the world, including Harvard, MIT, and the University of Massachusetts.

CHAPTER TWO

THE CURRENT
BOOM

A Gamble That Paid Off

Earlier in Kevin Starr's career, he served in various executive roles at Biogen and Digital Equipment Corporation. He was also chief operating officer and chief financial officer at Millennium Pharmaceuticals, where he helped raise billions of dollars in capital through strategic alliances and public financing and drove the company's growth through expansion, mergers, and acquisitions. While at Millennium, he and Mark Levin, a biochemical engineer who was previously with Eli Lilly and Genentech, worked together to market Velcade, a multiple myeloma drug.

According to an article in *Fortune,* in 2006, Starr and Levin made their annual gambling trip to Las Vegas, where they complained to each other about the drug industry's reputation of putting profits ahead of patients. Appropriately enough, on that trip—the focus of which was gambling—the idea for Third Rock Ventures was born.[18]

Robert Tepper, a former oncologist at Massachusetts General Hospital who headed research and development at Millennium, soon joined Starr and Levin for what would be Third Rock Ventures, a Boston-based venture capital firm.

In the early 2000s, even the best innovations failed to move beyond scholarly journals because of scarce funding. Aware of the prohibitive costs of taking a drug to market, the three men agreed that they would create and build businesses from scratch. Despite skepticism in the industry, after ten weeks, Third Rock had raised $378 million.

Today, the company's investments are very selective. As Third Rock's website states: "We discover, launch, and build great companies based on bold ideas that meet at the intersection of science, strategy,

---

18   Jennifer Alsever, "Third Rock Ventures: Giving Birth to a New Generation of Biotechs," Fortune, February 19, 2015, http://fortune.com/2015/02/19 third-rock-ventures-giving-birth-to-a-new-generation-of-biotechs/.

business, and medicine—where transformational science meets operational reality—providing the best opportunity to make a dramatic difference in patients' lives."[19]

The Biotech Ecosystem

Third Rock's story is an example of how entrepreneurs have thrived in the flourishing Massachusetts biotech ecosystem.

The boom ripples out, as if with tentacles, touching on numerous facets of commerce. There's a vibrancy in the economy and most of the state is experiencing a renaissance. The biotechnology industry has put Boston and Massachusetts on the map in a way that they never were in the past. When I started in my career, biotech stocks would soar and abruptly crash. Now, I can see that the industry has definitely affirmed itself. The Massachusetts legislature recently approved a $500 million grant for the biotech industry. Because of the grant, researchers are advancing rapidly in developing cutting-edge gene and stem cell therapies, bone graft substitute implants, and treatments for end-stage renal disease and acute kidney failure, among other innovations.

"By pretty much any measure, we are considered the leading life sciences ecosystem in the U.S., and among the leading ecosystems in the world," Travis McCready, CEO of the Massachusetts Life Sciences Center, told an *Associated Press* reporter.[20]

A top goal of the program, McCready said, is to develop the next generation of researchers. Currently, the center funds more than five hundred life sciences internships each year. Approximately one-

---

19   "Philosophy," Third Rock Ventures, accessed January 2019, http://www.thirdrockventures.com/investment-strategy/.

20   Steve LeBlanc, "10-Year, $10B Life Sciences Plan Bears Fruit in Massachusetts," Associated Press, August 17, 2017, https://www.apnews.com/4aa730649e8d44e28e9a43041c7e301c.

fourth of those interns are hired for full-time jobs at the companies where they interned. The talent pool is critical to biomanufacturing and digital health, the next stage in the life science revolution.[21]

Not all grant recipients will succeed, McCready acknowledged. "Some of these startups are going to fail, but ideas will be tested, and intellectual property will be created," he said. "Failure is not a negative."[22]

Education and research facilities, top-flight hospitals, government policy and investment, and a robust venture capital and angel investing atmosphere have created a perfect environment for that ecosystem to grow and flourish.

In a 2017 *Boston Globe* editorial, Dr. Jeffrey Leiden, chairman, president, and CEO of Vertex Pharmaceuticals, and Dr. David Torchiana, president and CEO of Partners HealthCare, stated, "There is no better example of the power of the innovation produced by this biomedical ecosystem than Massachusetts, which is the envy of the world. This network of leading teaching hospitals, universities, entrepreneur communities, venture capitalists and biotechnology companies, within 30 miles of each other, has created tremendous advances in healthcare and produced significant economic growth for the Commonwealth … This system employs more than 65,000 people."[23]

This is what the biotech money is doing. It's creating an expansive, productive, and thriving ecosystem!

---

21   Ibid.
22   Ibid.
23   Jeffrey Leiden and David Torchiana, "Nurturing the Biomedical Ecosystem," *Boston Globe,* May 16, 2017, https://www.bostonglobe.com/opinion/2017/05/15/nurturing-biomedical-ecosystem/fCX4cshHC0kCrllLcIr74M/story.html.

A Biotech Hub

Boston and the San Francisco Bay Area have the largest concentration of biotech activity in the world, and almost half of all investment in the industry takes place in these two areas. Approximately one-quarter of biotech companies in the US and one-third of biotech employees are located in one of the two areas. Depending on how you look at the numbers, Massachusetts—especially Boston and Cambridge—ranks either first or second among the world's biotech hubs. At the beginning of 2016, *Bloomberg Businessweek* rated Massachusetts the number one state for innovation, because of promising startups such as Editas Medicine, CRISPR Therapeutics, Intellia, and Bluebird Bio, all of which focus on gene editing, one of the fastest-growing biotech areas.[24]

"MassBio's annual industry snapshot makes clear Massachusetts is the #1 biotech cluster in the world, home to the best universities, hospitals, and biopharma companies, along with the brightest minds in the industry—but we didn't get there by chance," said MassBio President and CEO Robert K. Coughlin. "In order to remain on top, we must continue to foster a welcoming environment for life sciences companies to grow and move here. Governor Baker's recent announcement of a 5-year, $500 million life sciences '2.0' initiative is evidence that the state remains committed to the industry. As long as government, industry and academia continue to work together, we will maintain our stature."[25]

---

24   Michelle Jamrisko and Wei Lu, "Here are the Most Innovative States in America in 2016," *Bloomberg Businessweek,* December 22, 2016, https://www.bloomberg.com/news/articles/2016-12-22/here-are-the-most-innovative-states-in-america-in-2016.

25   Massachusetts Biotechnology Council, "MassBio's 2017 Industry Snapshot Shows Venture Capital Investment in Massachusetts Biopharma Industry Reached a Record $2.9 Billion Last Year," October 17, 2017, https://www.massbio.org/news/recent-news/massbio-s-2017-industry-snapshot-shows-venture-capital-investment-in-massachusetts-biopharma-industry-reached-a-record-2-9-billion-last-year-137592.

The Massachusetts Biotechnology Council also found the following:[26]

- There were fifteen IPOs from Massachusetts biotech companies between January and July of 2017.

- Massachusetts researchers were currently researching and developing products for patients with more than 380 different medical indications.

- In 2016, 25 percent of all drugs approved for orphan designation in the US were from Massachusetts companies.

Furthermore, in 2017, twelve of the state's biotech companies went public, representing 48 percent of all US-based biotech IPOs.[27] The presence of large drug companies like Shire, Sanofi Genzyme, and Biogen provide startups in the area with buyers, and, like the region's academic institutions, provide talent to startups and places for startup talent to go for new career opportunities. The largest employers in the sector are big pharma companies that are either headquartered in Massachusetts or have a significant presence there. Sanofi Genzyme and Biogen, two companies with their roots in the first wave of Massachusetts biotechs, lead the pack, employing 5,000 and 2,900 people, respectively.[28]

Five of the top six NIH-funded independent hospitals are in Massachusetts. Nonprofits such as Harvard Medical School, the Broad Institute, and UMass Medical School receive hundreds of

---

26   Massachusetts Biotechnology Council, "Industry Snapshot 2017," accessed January 2019, http://files.massbio.org/file/MassBio-Industry-Snapshot-2017.pdf.
27   Massachusetts Biotechnology Council, "2018 Industry Snapshot," accessed January 2019, http://files.massbio.org/file/MassBio-2018-Industry-Snapshot-FINAL-8-29-18.pdf.
28   Taylor Hardy, "Move over California – Boston is now the world's No.1 biotech hub," May 1, 2018, https://www.phaidoninternational.com/industryinsights/move-over-california-boston-is-now-the-worlds-no1-biotech-hub-81222193246.

millions of dollars from NIH. Massachusetts receives 57 percent of all NIH funding to independent hospitals.[29]

America's biopharmaceutical research companies had 901 biotechnology medicines and vaccines in development to target more than 100 debilitating and life-threatening diseases—such as cancer, arthritis, and diabetes—as far back at 2011, according to a report by the Pharmaceutical Research and Manufacturers of America (PhRMA).[30] The medicines in development—all in either clinical trials or under Food and Drug Administration review—included 353 for cancer and related conditions, 187 for infectious diseases, 69 for autoimmune diseases, and 59 for cardiovascular diseases.[31] Today, Massachusetts companies have 2,116 drug candidates, representing 16 percent of the US pipeline and 6 percent of the global pipeline.[32]

Outside Cambridge

Although Cambridge is certainly the center of all that activity, other areas of the state have grown their share of successful biotech startups. Half of the Massachusetts companies that went public in 2017 were from areas outside Cambridge.

The Worcester area is one of those hotspots. Worcester and its surroundings are home to more than fifty biotechnology companies, ranging from small startups to outposts for pharmaceutical giants such as AbbVie, the Illinois-based maker of rheumatoid arthritis drug Humira. At one point in 2016, 1,104 job openings in the industry were available in that area—second only to Cambridge at

29 Massachusetts Biotechnology Council, "2018 Industry Snapshot," op cit.
30 PhRMA, "Biotechnology presented by America's biopharmaceutical research companies," 2011, accessed January 2019, http://phrma-docs.phrma.org/sites/default/files/pdf/biotech2011.pdf.
31 Ibid.
32 Massachusetts Biotechnology Council, "2018 Industry Snapshot," op cit.

the time. The area ranks third in the state for the number of biotech companies.[33]

Nine of the area's colleges and universities offer degrees in life sciences and/or health-care. All told, the city is home to eighteen colleges and universities with more than ten new science buildings and thirty-five thousand students. UMass Medical School, the professional home of Nobel Prize winner Dr. Craig Mello, is a major player in research and a hub for life sciences companies. It was ranked 29th out of 139 US medical schools in NIH funding, according to the 2016 report from the Blue Ridge Institute for Medical Research. Ten academic departments at the school ranked in the top fifty among their peers at similarly named departments at US medical schools. UMMS received more than $143 million in NIH funding between October 1, 2015, and September 30, 2016, placing it among the top public medical schools in the Northeast, with its overall research funding from all sources being $288 million.[34]

The medical school is also home to UMass Medicine Science Park, a ten-acre plot adjacent to the campus. The Medicine Science Park includes 470,000 square feet of office and lab space and is home to dozens of biotech companies ranging in size from very early stage startups to larger players.

All this activity leads to a system with plenty of rewards. *US News & World Report* recently ranked Worcester 62 out of 125 cities of similar size it deemed best places to live.[35] *Forbes* ranked it 10 out

---

33   Livia Gershon, "Biotech is putting people to work in the Central Mass. 100," May 23, 2016, http://www.wbjournal.com/article/20160523/PRINTEDITION/305209983/ biotech-is-putting-people-to-work-in-the-central-mass-100.

34   Lisa M. Larson, "UMMS ranks in top 25 percent of medical schools in NIH funding; departments score high against peers," February 6, 2017, https://www.umassmed.edu/ news/news-archives/2017/01/umass-medical-school-ranks-in-top-25-percent-of-medical-schools-in-nih-funding/.

35   "125 Best Places to Live in the USA," US News and World Report, 2018, https://realestate. usnews.com/places/rankings/best-places-to-live.

of 100 large metro-cities for best places to raise a family.[36] Rewards bring the responsibility to set goals and plan for the future. In their *Boston Globe* opinion piece, Leiden and Torchiana concluded by saying, "The cost of not investing in innovation is clear. However, if we properly nurture and support the innovation ecosystem, we are confident that Massachusetts can continue to lead the way, creating cures and preventive therapies for serious diseases and bending the cost curve for the U.S. healthcare system, all while fostering economic growth and new jobs for our local and national economy."[37]

Your Human Capital

Some people—both potential employees and investors—might prefer to approach the industry from a more stable standpoint and choose larger, well-established pharmaceutical or medical device companies. Although they are going to be rewarded for their efforts with more job security and predictability, they may not have as great an upside as somebody who is involved in a startup or recent IPO.

Career path decisions have risks and rewards similar to investments. To clarify this, where you derive your economic value from, or simply your income and employee benefits from, is referred to as your human capital. Choosing a more stable, well-established employer is like investing in a bond. You go in knowing it is safer, predictable, and steady. As long as you perform your duties competently, you have a pretty good idea of what you're going to have at the end, but you're probably not going get rich overnight. Startup companies are definitely riskier. Founders and executives derive their human capital from owning, and being incentivized by, company

---

36   "Best Cities for Raising a Family," *Forbes,* accessed January 2019, https://www.forbes.com/pictures/eddf45gihi/best-cities-for-raising-a-family/#4141c1832bb3.
37   Leiden and Torchiana, op. cit.

stock. Most often early hires will be enticed to join a startup via stock options or restricted stock, and the payoff is that when the company succeeds, they will be rewarded upon a successful liquidity event, such as an IPO or acquisition by a big pharma company. The payoffs can be enormous and life changing.

So, yes there is a big upside, and there are risks that we'll dive into in later chapters. There also is some stability, and we'll later look at ways to approach that as well.

Some early biotech entrepreneurs have been able to cash in, and some haven't. Some ended up making a lot of money and went on to start more companies. Some started or joined venture capital companies that invest in early-stage startups. Others who haven't cashed in may be looking for something more stable and predictable to secure a future retirement for themselves. The beauty of a career, and investing in this industry, is that it covers the full spectrum from safety to speculation. The key is to know how your human capital can affect your personal finances, both positively and negatively.

Entrepreneur, Executive, or Scientist?

Regardless of how you see yourself being employed within the life sciences industry, you can expect certain financial rewards. As mentioned, with the onslaught of these new companies, founders, executives, and key scientific employees are going to be incentivized monetarily to perform. That generally takes the form of equity, such as restricted stock, restricted stock units (RSUs), or stock options. Restricted stock and RSUs are more popular than stock options today. How you manage these grants is critical to your personal financial success. Decisions must be made surrounding these benefits, such as the impact of income and estate taxes, concentrated positions and stock market risk, blackout periods, insider information, business and economic environments, and the health and prospects of the company itself.

Generally, upper management is rewarded, or penalized, by the performance of the company's stock. However, top executives may also have a significant salary along with retirement plans like 401(k)s and nonqualified deferred compensation plans; life, health, and disability insurance; and flexible spending accounts. These executives and entrepreneurs, with their various plans and much-needed strategies to implement them, are the focus of our work at Peak Financial.

As those benefits are taken advantage of, they should be approached in a uniform manner and as a whole. For example, in anticipation of one's restricted stock vesting or exercising stock options, an executive might balance that by taking advantage of a nonqualified deferred compensation plan to soften the tax hit from those events. We'll elaborate on these strategies in later chapters.

As these benefits go into effect, a large portion of individuals' net worth could be concentrated in the stock of their employer or their company. Their human capital becomes more and more dependent on the performance of that one company. Thus, we introduce our clients to strategies that mitigate the market risks and potential tax burdens that can come along with these concentrated positions. These strategies allow them to divest of these concentrated positions systematically, cost effectively, and tax efficiently, while complementing their overall personal financial plans.

Should I Stay or Should I Go?

Excellent employees are often offered outstanding incentives and advancements, and leaving can be difficult for them. However, if they have a comprehensive plan taking into consideration their future retirement lifestyle or other goals, our process will help them understand how much in investable assets they will need to generate income to secure their lifestyle and fulfill their dreams, goals, and objectives. This can mean the difference between hanging on too long or truly enjoying the fruits of their labor.

Most of our clients have a greater purpose in life than just making money. They may be charitably inclined and want to make an impact reflecting their vision and values. We incorporate charitable giving strategies into the plans of these clients. That strategy can also serve to divest of their concentrated stock positions in a most tax-efficient manner, while still complementing short- and long-term goals.

Depending on the individual goals and values of our clients, our job is to customize plans that meet their needs. Many of our clients want to take care of family members. Others just want to be "secure." Our five-step comprehensive wealth management process helps to define goals, navigate toward them, and reach them.

What's the Number?

What is the number you need to live on? Is it $20 million, $10 million, $5 million, or $2 million? Is it worth another $800,000 or $1 million to work another two or three years, or are you better off just saying, "All right, enough is enough. I am going to enjoy my life and not have to work anymore."? Basically, what is your exit strategy?

The bottom line is this: there is a boom in the life sciences market and tremendous rewards await, both scientifically and monetarily.

There are few better places to start figuring this out than in the rapidly growing and evolving atmosphere of the Massachusetts biotechnology and life sciences cluster. The bottom line is this: there is a boom in the life sciences market and tremendous rewards await, both scientifically and monetarily. So if you possess the knowledge, skills, and work ethic to perform, and if you want to gain the clarity and confidence to navigate this space successfully, please take advantage of our complimentary Second Opinion Service at http://www.peakfs.com/p/comprehensive-wealth-management-process.

In chapter 5 we are going to dive into planning your financial future. First, though, it's important for you to understand the ripples and risks of the boom from an entrepreneurial standpoint. Next, we're going to look at the ripples, including an entrepreneur named Dennis Guberski, whose company has been experiencing 45 to 50 percent growth over the past six years.

Takeaway

- The biotechnology industry has put Boston and Massachusetts on the map in a way that they never were in the past.

- Although Cambridge is certainly the center of all that activity, other areas of the state have grown their share of successful biotech startups.

- Opting to work for a more stable and well-established company can be similar to investing in a bond: it's predictable and fairly steady.

- Being employed with a startup or recent IPO company is more like investing in the stock market: it's riskier and less predictable, but has potentially greater rewards.

CHAPTER THREE

RIPPLES OF THE BOOM

In 1996, Dennis Guberski and a few colleagues founded Bio-technology Medical Research, Inc. (now Biomere) in Worcester as a spinoff of UMass Medical School. The $900,000 in loans they used to start the company came from the Massachusetts Development Finance Agency and the city of Worcester, along with investments from a group Guberski called DDFs—doctors, dentists, friends, family, and fools! I spoke with him recently on his experience with and thoughts on the biotech industry; much of this chapter is the result of that discussion.

The dilapidated fifteen thousand square-foot building Guberski rented was soon transformed into a gleaming, high-tech laboratory. They hired two accountants as partners, while Guberski and his colleagues focused on their core competencies as geneticists and research scientists. They began with a contract from Eli Lilly to test insulin delivery systems and drugs. Along the way, they attracted small business research grants.

Biomere is an example of how a "picks and shovels" type of company within the biotech space can flourish. Instead of doing its own research and developing its own drugs, Biomere is considered a Contract Research Organization, or CRO. It performs preclinical or FDA testing for other startups. By outsourcing many facets of a business, individual scientists can research and discover therapies more cost effectively and efficiently. This has sped up the process for bringing drugs to market. Rather than creating whole multidepartmental companies around ideas, scientists can patent their ideas, outsource business functions, and remain committed to and focused on the process of creating successful therapeutic solutions that can then be commercialized.

Guberski's company has been experiencing 45 to 50 percent growth most recently and has expanded to employ more than seventy people in 2017. Guberski said he can perform testing that is less costly than in the Boston-Cambridge area. In fact, his company in Worcester can perform tests for about $100,000 less than a company in the biotech epicenter of Cambridge.

A recognized expert on the development and maintenance of specialized research models, including a premier system to study diabetic complications, Guberski was selected by NIH to participate in a task force to develop a national genetic resource repository for laboratory rats. He also served on the scientific review board for the NIH Autoimmune Rat Repository in Bethesda, Maryland.

His objective has always been to grow the company to a point where he can sell it to a larger lab or another entrepreneur. He has arranged to have his employees also benefit from that by establishing stock in trust for them down the road.

Guberski both believes in and is evidence of the benefits of Worcester and the larger Massachusetts biotech ecosystem. Biomere has gained a great deal through its proximity to top medical schools and research facilities. He points out that 15 of the nation's 125 medical schools are within three hours of his hometown.

Dennis Guberski's story is the kind I like to tell because he is an example of how business owners have thrived in the flourishing Massachusetts biotech ecosystem. Many of those with whom I spoke for this book also have benefitted from the ripples of biotechnology. In chapter 1, I mentioned how Third Rock Ventures was founded. I interviewed Kevin Gillis, Third Rock partner and chief financial officer.

A Novel Approach to Creating Biotech Companies

Today, Third Rock's partners each work with only two companies at a time. As Gillis said, "What we do is basically outsource innovation." As a partner in a VC firm with a portfolio of several companies, Gillis's human capital risk is reduced compared to an entrepreneur or executive working for only one company.

One of Third Rock's macro themes is making a big difference for patients. As touched on earlier, that was a major reason the company was founded. Gillis and his partners seek "more nimble biotech companies." Via lab tours at academic powerhouses like MIT and Harvard, Third Rock acts as a conduit for academia, approaching big pharma with state-of-the-art, cutting-edge ideas.

Third Rock's mission "is to be the preferred partner for entrepreneurs, investors, employees and industry to build great companies that discover and develop products that make a difference for the patients we serve." And further: "We take a long-term approach to company building, creating a portfolio of companies with the potential to make a dramatic difference in patients' lives. Our unique Discover, Launch, Build process brings together the best inside and outside experts, allocates capital and resources based on where an idea or company is in its development and provides our companies with the support necessary to advance novel therapies, devices and diagnostics."[38]

Before any company obtains full funding from Third Rock, it must go through a due diligence period, which can take one to two years. Many ideas are "killed" in the early stages of due diligence, according to Gillis. If a company passes this phase, Third Rock will

---

38   "Our Mission," Third Rock Ventures, http://www.thirdrockventures.com/mission-and-core-values/.

take on 100 percent of the Series A round financing, putting up an average of $40 to $60 million, spread over two to three tranches, based on the achievement of pre-stated performance goals. This approach has garnered Third Rock and its investors an approximately 40 percent success rate versus the industry average of 10 percent, Gillis told me.

A great example of the old blended with the new. Alexandria Real Estate Equities acquired One Kendall Square in November 2016 from DivcoWest for $725 million, or $1,124 per square foot. DivcoWest acquired One Kendall Square in January 2014 for $395 million, or $613 per square foot.

Unlike the early days of biotechnology, where an entire company would be built around a product or two, we now have smaller outsourced consultancy companies that complement the entire process. Thus, a company in which Third Rock or others invest doesn't have to build an entire nuts-and-bolts organization. These startups now can outsource specific tasks and processes to contract resource organizations (CROs). Hence, the "burn rate" of investable capital has been minimized dramatically.

Favorable Environment for Entrepreneurs

Tom Andrews, a co-president and regional market director at Alexandria Real Estate Equities, Inc., with whom I also spoke, focuses on the company's overall strategic operations and leads its Greater Boston asset base and operations. Andrews has steered the growth of Greater Boston into the company's largest region, which includes the prominent life science and technology campuses, Alexandria Technology Square, Alexandria Center at Kendall Square, and Alexandria Center at One Kendall Square, in the heart of Cambridge. The company is responsible for a large number of labs and space rented by biotechs.

"It's a very favorable environment for entrepreneurs today," Andrews told me. "Regulators have become more accommodating and are collaborating with industries. The ability [for entrepreneurs] to analyze large data is more efficient."

One of the reasons for this is what Gillis refers to above as companies becoming "nimble."

According to Andrews, approvals have become a little easier. The Food and Drug Administration is listening more to patient advocates, and this has led to more product approvals. Pharma businesses have started to be more receptive to licensing with small firms, investing in startups, and partnering with these companies and other investors. As a result, the synergism among these different levels is more pronounced, and endowments, foundations, and pension funds are investing more as well.

Andrews sees a "long tail of continued opportunity." This progress will continue for many years in the future.

"There are ten thousand human ailments," he said. "We have cures for five hundred of them."

With that said, Massachusetts-headquartered companies have developed therapies that treat patient populations of up to 264,450,000 in the US and 1,989,571,000 around the world.[39]

More Collaboration, Outsourcing

In the past, academia, venture capitalists, and investors coexisted in a more competitive environment. Today, they are collaborating. The academic world is sharing more of its research, and VCs and big pharma work more closely together. Industry-specific conferences around the world are facilitating "partnering" sessions, where founders of startups can meet directly with CEOs and business development decision makers of VCs and big pharma to pitch their ideas in prescheduled private gatherings. The Biotechnology Innovation Organization's 2018 Conference in Boston set a Guinness World Record for "The Largest Business Partnering Event" with 46,916 partnering meetings taking place over four days.

As I write this book, Alexandria Real Estate is launching Alexandria LaunchLabs in One Kendall Square. Building upon the success of the initial Alexandria LaunchLabs site, which opened at the Alexandria Center for Life Science in New York in 2017, the company has brought its Alexandria LaunchLabs platform to Cambridge to meet the cluster's demand for life science startup space. Again, we see the "nimble" trend, where one startup doesn't have to include every aspect of the business in one company.

According to Andrews, the LaunchLabs will provide member companies with more than twenty thousand square feet of col-

---

39　Massachusetts Biotechnology Council, "Industry Snapshot 2017," op. cit.

laborative coworking space. Flexible shared or private offices and fully-permitted, plug-and-play shared laboratories as well as shared equipment and services will be more cost effective than going it alone as companies in the past had to do. Adaptable, private laboratory configurations will allow companies to expand into contiguous laboratory suites, and dedicated tissue culture suites are available.

The facility also offers state-of-the-art conferencing amenities, mentorship, and highly curated programming. An on-site management team with a strong background in life science, laboratory operations, entrepreneurship, venture capital, and investor relations will provide member companies with resources to enhance their growth trajectories.

Members will also have the opportunity to access seed capital and mentorship through the Alexandria Seed Capital Platform, a funding model that brings together leaders from across the life science community to catalyze seed-stage investment in promising life science startups. The Alexandria Seed Capital Platform is led by Alexandria Venture Investments and supported by an advisory board of biopharma and venture capital executives from Accelerator Life Science Partners, ARCH Venture Partners, Eli Lilly and Company, Pfizer, and Roche.

Orphan Diseases: A More Efficient Timeline

As the market ripples, orphan diseases are another segment, one that William Duke, Jr., CFO of Pulmatrix, told me in an interview is more efficient getting to market. The Lexington, Massachusetts-based clinical-stage biopharmaceutical company develops innovative inhaled therapies to address serious pulmonary disease. The proprietary product pipeline is focused on advancing treatments for rare diseases. Products include PUR1900, an inhaled antifungal for patients with lung disease, including cystic fibrosis. In addition, Pulmatrix is pursuing opportunities in major pulmonary diseases through collaboration with partners, including PUR0200, a branded generic in clinical development for chronic obstructive pulmonary disease.

An orphan disease is defined as a condition that affects fewer than two hundred thousand people nationwide. This includes cystic fibrosis, Lou Gehrig's disease, and Tourette's syndrome, and it also includes less-familiar ailments such as Hamburger disease and acromegaly, or "gigantism." It can also be common diseases like tuberculosis, malaria, typhoid, and cholera that have been ignored because they are far more prevalent in developing countries than in the developed world. Twenty-five percent of orphan drugs approved from US-based companies in 2016 were from companies headquartered in Massachusetts.

The average time frame is ten years to get a drug to market, so being more efficient saves both time and money, especially considering that big pharma waits until products are farther along before getting financially involved.

Medical Device Manufacturing

"Then" Coghlin Companies

A fourth-generation, family-owned business that dates back to 1885, Coghlin Companies originated in Worcester. The founder, John P. Coghlin, was an electrical engineer and a graduate of Worcester Polytechnical Institute (WPI). At first the company was responsible for many power and electrical projects throughout the city of Worcester and surrounding towns. Subsequent generations of Coghlins continued this tradition and began to see an opportunity to do high-tech, military, and medical device contract manufacturing starting in the 1990s. With the cost of in-house manufacturing now prohibitive for many companies, today, through its subsidiaries Columbia Tech and Cogmedix, Coghlin Companies provides turn-key manufacturing services to a broad range of innovative medical and dental original equipment manufacturers (OEMs). The company's primary focus is on complex electro-mechanical and electro-optical devices, as well as laser-based technologies. Just as biotechnology has had a positive impact on patients' lives, Coghlin Companies is helping to create true life-enhancing devices. Its collaboration with Myomo, for example, allows it to develop FDA-approved, custom-fitted orthoses that facilitate functional tasks and patient independence.

"Now" Coghlin Companies

I interviewed James (Jim) W. Coghlin, Jr., vice chairman and chief supply chain officer of Coghlin Companies. Jim is from the younger generation of the Coghlin family. He and his brother, Chris, who is the CEO of Coghlin Companies, saw the opportunity for high-tech and medical device manufacturing. They created these companies specifically to carve out market share and participate in this market. In doing so, they took an older economy-type company and transformed and expanded it into these new economy manufacturing companies. Coghlin Companies is a tremendous example of how the life sciences industry has allowed old and new companies alike to thrive and expand as the ripples of the boom continue on.

Hiring and Keeping Younger Employees

It's no secret that millennials have different values and career expectations than the generations before them.

"Our company refers to employees as *caring associates,* and Chris or I are an *executive sponsor* for each customer," Coghlin told me. He is addressing, in part, the issues and concerns of younger employees, who think differently than baby boomers, for instance. Leisure and flexible hours are important to them. So are enjoying a fun environment and working as a team as opposed to individuals competing amongst each other. Coghlin said his younger employees thrive in an environment with "lots of communication, flat screen informative TVs, external social events, and company events."

Companies like the Coghlin's look to find potential employees when they're still in college. They provide summer internships and training programs. Even before that, they work with the schools to prepare the students. Again, success in the industry results from a collaborative effort between academia and industry.

Although Coghlin hires many younger employees today, the firm's initial breakthroughs into medical devices came through hiring experienced personnel. These hires came with networks of contacts, experience, and the vision to see the future of the industries Columbia Tech and Cogmedix would thrive in.

The biotech industry has found success in providing the work-hard, play-hard environment many in this age group prefer. These companies also appeal to the group's sense of community and desire to work for a purpose as much as a paycheck. Many companies also provide great flexibility.

That's important, because flexibility is one of the central priorities for millennial workers, according to a 2018 opinion piece in *International Business Times*: "This generation prefers work when given detailed instructions and set KPIs (Key Performance Indicators) but would prefer to have a flexible working arrangement to being micromanaged," author Oliver Cooke writes. "Flexible working environments are also attractive to millennials looking to keep a work-life balance. Millennials value the potential to work from home or remotely with the emphasis being on the quality of work, rather than the location where the work is performed."[40]

Less Commuting

In the past five to ten years, people have preferred to live in the city, Andrews told me. Today, they would rather live away from the city.

---

40   Oliver Cooke, "How to Create the Best Workplace for Millennials in 2018," *International Business Times*, January 10, 2018, http://www.ibtimes.com/how-create-best-workplace-millennials-2018-2639847.

They also want less commuting, which means finding work closer to home.

Jonathan Freve started in public accounting with PwC, consulting with biotech companies. It was a stable career and a great avenue to get started in the industry. At this writing, he has been working in biotech for fifteen years.

He and his wife were in public accounting and he decided to go into corporate accounting to diversify their sources of income. On the public accounting side, he couldn't invest in the company he was auditing, and he was seeing people make millions, so he made a calculated risk to get out of public accounting and get into Brookfield Renewable Energy, an IT company, as their corporate controller. Then, he worked at Syntaris for one year, where he received stock options. When Syntaris was bought by Roche, he benefitted financially.

"There are so many opportunities for helping society with cures," he told me when I interviewed him for this book. "It's a young, vibrant industry, with lots of change and innovations. Yet, there's stability within the industry because there are so many opportunities."

He said he is attracted to the congenial environment, the leadership, the vibrant social scene, and the cultural thread of having fun, working hard, and playing hard.

He works in Hopkinton, which is the town where the Boston Marathon starts every year. Hopkinton, located twenty-seven miles from Boston, is attracting talent because of the reverse commute. Venture capitalists want to be close to their companies, which means they would prefer them to be downtown in Cambridge, and closer to them.

Yet Hopkinton comes with significantly lower rents than those of Kendall Square, and those commuters coming out of the city aren't bogged down in the morning because the traffic is all going into the city.

Andrews, of Alexandria Real Estate, predicts that the bio manufacturing facilities will be located in suburbs because the land cost and security are more affordable than in the city. Worcester is making a big push to become a bio manufacturing center because its roots are in manufacturing.

Because of the state's rich history in biotechnology, many of its communities have continued to adopt local policies that greatly lower the barriers to renovation or new construction of biotech laboratory and manufacturing facilities. They have done this with the support of state government. MassBio has developed BioReady ratings for municipalities that submit details on their zoning practices and infrastructure capacity.

The industry is not a dot or two on a map of Massachusetts. It is a moving current, and each area has its advantages, ranging from cost of living and working to commute time. On the west side, known as the Knowledge Corridor, you'll find UMass-Amherst and twenty-one other colleges. The immediate western suburbs of Boston-Cambridge include more than seventy-five biotech companies, fifteen colleges, and three million square feet of lab space. Next is Worcester, with more than fifty biotech companies, Worcester Polytechnic Institute, UMass Medical Center, and sixteen other colleges. In the northeast, you'll find more than fifty biotech companies, more than two million square feet of lab space, UMass-Lowell, and eleven other colleges.

Then, you have the Boston-Cambridge area—home of Vertex, Sanofi, Biogen, and Novartis—with more than five hundred biotech companies, the five of the top six NIH-funded hospitals in the US, and forty-eight colleges. The south coast has a strong medical device and biopharma manufacturing capacity and has numerous land sites in BioReady communities. It also has ten colleges.

The Ripple Continues

The 2018 "Job Trends Forecast" from the Massachusetts Biotechnology Education Foundation makes it clear that the ripple isn't diminishing in the least. The forecast, which provides an overview of hiring demands in the life sciences industry in Massachusetts, as well as projections of employment growth by sector and occupation, also includes findings from MassBioEd's annual survey of industry employers, which gathered input from hiring decision makers at life sciences organizations on workforce matters most pressing to them.[41]

"After another year of healthy employment growth for the industry, MassBioEd forecasts continued robust hiring by the industry," said Peter Abair, executive director of MassBioEd. "Looking closely at the supply and demand dynamics of the workforce, it's clear we need to grow the available pool of talent from which the industry can draw employees, which can be best supported by improving the alignment of education programs with the skills required by employers and by industry increasing early career experiences for students."[42]

According to the report, the life sciences industry exceeded seventy thousand employees for the first time, showing the incredible growth that continues. Key findings include the fact that, since 2014, employment in the life sciences industry in Massachusetts has grown at approximately *double* the rate of the state and US economy.

---

41   "MassBioEd Releases 2018 Job Trends Forecast for Life Sciences Industry in Massachusetts," Massachusetts Biotechnology Education Foundation, May 16, 2018, https://www.massbioed. org/news/174-massbioed-releases-2018-job-trends-forecast-for-life-sciences-industry-in-massa- chusetts.
42   Ibid.

In 2017, the total amount of job listings exceeded 27,700, second only to 2016. Of those, STEM/technical jobs accounted for more than 16,000.[43]

A total of 11,976 new jobs are forecast to be created between May 2017 and May 2023. Eighty-three percent of life sciences companies reported plans to expand their head count in the next twelve months, consistent with the previous two years.[44]

The report also highlighted several challenges this growth presents for life sciences organizations, including the fact that 65 percent of organizations reported that the average time it took to fill openings was more than ten weeks. Considering that the national average is approximately thirty days, one can see that the industry can use more training and more qualified candidates. A total of 31 percent listed clinical research as the hardest area in which to find qualified candidates. This was followed by openings in regulatory affairs, quality, and research and development roles. These are also the top four functional areas in which life sciences organizations are planning to expand in 2018.[45]

In job openings that required at least an associate's degree and up to a PhD, again, both areas saw much higher levels of growth in demand than supply. Twenty-nine percent of respondents stated that their companies had formal diversity initiatives for either gender or race/ethnicity at the contributor level and 28 percent at the management level. At the board level, the rate dropped to only 17 percent of companies. About 60 percent of companies reported lacking any formal diversity initiatives.[46]

---

43 Ibid.
44 Ibid.
45 Ibid.
46 Ibid.

Choosing a Career Path

As mentioned in chapter 2, in biotech as in any field, deciding on a career path comes down to personality and personal values. As an entrepreneur of a startup, your path is somewhat predestined. You can discover a novel drug for an existing ailment or expand upon existing intellectual property to deliver a therapeutic method more effectively or efficiently to a larger patient population. Whichever way you go, as an entrepreneur, you are effectively a business owner and an officer of the company. This comes with added risks and responsibilities compared to a scientist who is employed by big pharma or big bio.

On the other hand, as an executive, the choice can be to go with the security of an established pharmaceutical, biotechnology, or medical device company, or the high risk and potential rewards of a successful startup or recent IPO.

These are important life-altering decisions, and I want to be sure I convey this as people enter or change jobs within the industry. As you will see in the next chapter, although the rewards of startups are great, the failure rate is high. If you begin with one of the larger companies, you can learn all you need to, discover your strengths, and create a solid financial foundation for yourself. Then, you can afford to take the risk of going with the startups or recent IPOs. What if the one you pick fails? If you've created a solid financial foundation, you shouldn't be totally adversely affected. As you'll see in the next chapter, working for a failed startup is not a stigma in the biotech industry.

Going with the startup, as Duke points out, gives you the ability to gain different experience, which enhances your career marketability going forward. So, it's a calculated risk that can pay off now or later, regardless of what that startup does or doesn't do.

Jonathan Freve pointed out when we spoke that networking is key for career advancement. A placement service is second best, he said. What really matters are your connections. That's a theme you will see throughout this book. The biotech industry is large, but it's still local, and people know each other. On a national stage the industry is large, but it's made up of heavily concentrated hubs.

Takeaway

- Massachusetts-headquartered companies have developed therapies that treat patient populations of up to 264,450,000 in the US and 1,989,571,000 globally.

- The biotech industry has found success in providing the work-hard, play-hard environment many millennials prefer.

- Today, people in the industry don't want a long, congested commute. They also want to live both in and away from the city.

- Because of the state's rich history in biotechnology, many Massachusetts communities have continued to adopt local policies that greatly ease the pathway for renovation or new construction of biotech laboratory and manufacturing facilities.

- A total of 11,976 new life sciences jobs are forecast to be created in Massachusetts between May 2017 and May 2023.

- Going with a startup is a calculated risk with the potential to pay off now or later, regardless of the startup's ultimate fate.

CHAPTER FOUR

RIDING OVER THE ROUGH SPOTS

In 2008, Tolerx was named one of Fierce Biotech's "Fierce 15." Headquartered in Cambridge, Massachusetts, the company developed new therapies to treat patients by reprogramming the immune system, allowing for—after a short course of therapy— long-term remission of immune-related diseases. The company focused on patients suffering from rheumatoid arthritis, cancer, chronic and viral diseases, inflammatory bowel disease, and type 1 diabetes. All it needed was FDA approval. The Phase 3 trial in patients recently diagnosed with type 1 diabetes would be the beginning. With champagne already purchased, they waited for the good news.

It never came. The Phase 3 trial was unsuccessful. In October 2011, Tolerx was shut down overnight. That's an example of how quickly fortunes can be made and lost in biotech.

David Easson, now vice president of manufacturing technology transfer for Indigo Agriculture in Boston, started Worcester-based Alpha Beta Technology in 1988. In early 1992, the company started Phase 1 clinical trials of Betafectin, a carbohydrate-based compound under development for the treatment of infections related to surgery and cancer chemotherapy. It made it to Phase 3 clinical trials to prevent serious postoperative infection in GI surgical patients—for example, for Crohn's disease or ulcerative colitis.

A June 1997 article in *The Pharma Letter* states, "Alpha-Beta Technology's shares plunged 43 percent to $6.32 on the day the company disclosed disappointing preliminary data from a Phase 3 study of its carbohydrate drug Betafectin (PGG-glucan)."[47]

That was the beginning of the end. Another failure? That depends on how you look at it.

---

47   "Alpha Beta's Betafectin, Disappointing Ph III Data," *The Pharma Letter,* June 8, 1997, https://www.thepharmaletter.com/article/alpha-beta-s-betafectin-disappointing-ph-iii-data.

When Easson started out, entrepreneurs were able to get capital with just an idea. With an excellent educational background and work experience, not to mention a good idea, he was able to bring the drug public before it was even commercialized. But then, it failed the FDA testing.

It was a classic, publicly traded company, and he may have been pigeonholed into a single product. He wanted to develop a pipeline of opportunities, but there was too much pressure on getting that one, specific drug to market in a timely manner, and he was unable to diversify the pipeline.

In the world of biotechnology, companies can and do shut down overnight. A startup faces years of expensive research and development and then clinical trials. After all that, it still has to achieve FDA approval, as well as ascertain how it will produce a new drug in mass quantities. In that risky environment, you must have a plan to stay whole if a company doesn't pan out as expected. That is essential.

In a 2017 opinion piece for *Pharmaceutical Technology*, Chris Lo observed, "For a large pharma company such as Bristol-Myers Squibb—which announced the failure of a Phase 3 study of its cancer immunotherapy drug Opdivo in August [2016], sparking an eventual 35 percent drop in its share price—lost investments due to drug development failures can be absorbed to some extent. But for smaller firms, a single late-stage trial flunk can be disastrous. Biopharma firm NewLink Genetics was forced to lay off one hundred employees—43 percent of its total workforce—after the failure of a Phase 3 trial assessing its own immunotherapy treatment in May [2016]."[48]

Bill Duke, of Pulmatrix, said to me that we have to consider what is fair pricing for future products if we are going to improve

---

48   Chris Lo, "Counting the Cost of Failure in Drug Development," *Pharmaceutical Technology*, June 19, 2017, https://www.pharmaceutical-technology.com/features/featurecounting-the-cost-of-failure-in-drug-development-5813046/.

success rates. The US and the Food and Drug Administration have certain regulations that Europe doesn't. So, European companies can sell products cheaper and their single-payer system forces companies' hands. However, the US is still the preferred location for startups and to bring a drug to market, because of the potential profitability.

Developing a new prescription medicine that gains marketing approval is estimated to cost drugmakers $2.6 billion according to a recent study by Tufts Center for the Study of Drug Development. This is up from $802 million in 2003—equal to approximately $1 billion in 2013 dollars, and thus a 145 percent increase in the ten year study gap. Furthermore, while the average time it takes to bring a drug through clinical trials has decreased, the rate of success has gone down by almost half, to just 12 percent.[49]

Going forward the industry cannot rely solely on this fact to justify its pricing model. Government pressures and political maneuvering over pricing are on the rise. Companies may need to be more transparent for each therapeutic brought to market, pricing them accordingly on their own merits. This will most likely be a hot topic come the 2020 elections.

Resilience and Recoverability

Despite the demise of Alpha-Beta, Easson had many successes. He had the backing of MIT. He had some venture capital funding, and he did some public rounds. Because he had mezzanine funding, he was able to generate a lot of capital and backing. He took a company public, and when that company was no longer successful, he landed

---

49 Thomas Sullivan, "A Tough Road: Cost To Develop One New Drug Is $2.6 Billion; Approval Rate for Drugs Entering Clinical Development is Less Than 12%," May 6, 2018, https://www. policymed.com/2014/12/a-tough-road-cost-to-develop-one-new-drug-is-26-billion-approval-rate-for-drugs-entering-clinical-de.html.

on his feet. You can take some of these risks at certain points in your career. In the interim, he became the director of the WPI Life Sciences and Bioengineering Center and is now vice president of manufacturing technology transfer with Indigo Ag, a "unicorn" (a privately held startup company valued at over $1 billion) private life sciences company based in Boston.

Easson has a tremendous wealth of knowledge and experience because of Alpha-Beta. He was able to leverage that easily going forward because of demand for that type of experience and ability.

His experience is an example of the career resilience and recoverability the industry offers. Failure doesn't mean the end of a career. It means that you learned a lot in that process. Like Easson, you might learn how to take a company public or how to raise a lot of capital from various avenues. You still have the potential to rebound and recover from any setbacks because of the vast opportunities that exist.

"Many new startups begin at universities with support from big pharma," Easson told me in an interview. He also points out that "there are many new incubators that are service oriented and reduce the risks for these seed-stage startups."

As noted previously, the incubators provide different services. For the entrepreneur, being able to outsource a lot of the processes that go into bringing a drug to market can make the undertaking viable.

These incubators exist, of course, because the focus is on changing that statistic of nine failures to one success. The more expenses can be lowered and shared, the sooner the odds are going to improve, and more startups are going to succeed. In the meantime, employees and entrepreneurs need to be realistic about possible outcomes. They need to protect their wealth and plan for their future regardless of their current position—because if there is a constant in the world of biotech, it is that everything changes.

"Executives should have a plan to systematically divest," Easson told me. "Have a plan and set up a divesting system that is consistent."

Working with an Advisor

As an advisor, I am naturally biased in favor of my profession, but with that said, I think Duke made a good point when speaking to me about how working with a financial advisor helps to leverage his time and his expertise: "It helps me enjoy family time more and have a better work-life balance and peace of mind," he said.

In other words, he can be more productive while he is working, knowing that the money he has earned is going in the right places for what he really wants to accomplish personally.

Takeaway

- Risk is part of the business. Nine out of ten startups fail.[50]

- A startup faces years of expensive research and development and then clinical trials. After all that, it still has to achieve Food and Drug Administration approval, as well as ascertain how it will produce a new drug in mass quantities.

- We have to consider what is fair pricing for future products if we are going to improve success rates.

- Work-life balance is a challenge in the biotech industry.

- Biotech is an exciting but also very volatile business, and it requires a whole different level of financial planning.

---

50 Erin Griffith, "Why startups fail, according to their founders," Fortune, September 25, 2014, http://fortune.com/2014/09/25/why-startups-fail-according-to-their-founders/.

CHAPTER FIVE

IMPORTANCE OF THE WEALTH-MANAGEMENT PROCESS

Thus far in this book, we have looked at the biotechnology industry—the beginnings of the boom, the increasingly far-reaching ripples, and the ever-present risks. We've also seen how those who've been able to navigate the pitfalls have been positioned to make considerable fortunes. The next step is to look at how to manage that wealth.

Our Definition

Our definition of wealth management is threefold: **Wealth management (WM)** equals **investment consulting (IC)** plus **advanced planning (AP)** plus **relationship management (RM)**. WM = IC + AP + RM.

Investment Consulting

Virtually all financial advisors perform investment consulting. That involves evaluating the client's existing investment portfolio and determining its performance, how the assets are allocated, and assessing and addressing any tax issues the portfolio may create. If time has been taken to understand the client's short, intermediate, and long-term goals, along with their tolerance for risk, then an investment policy statement (IPS) should be created. Most people we see do not have a defined IPS, so we create one for them. If they already have an IPS, we review it and determine if it is in sync with their current portfolio allocations and risk tolerance level.

Advanced Planning

What differentiates us from many of our competitors is the following formula: Advanced planning (AP) *equals* wealth enhancement (WE) *plus* wealth transfer (WT) *plus* wealth protection (WP) *plus* charitable giving (CG). Once we've completed a thorough evaluation, you're ready to execute a plan of action. You wouldn't embark on a long trip through new territory without a detailed roadmap. Without that map, you might miss many opportunities—and you might wander into dangerous territory. The same is true of your financial journey. It's not enough to simply acquire wealth. You need to think ahead regarding how you can use the legal system and tax code to protect what you acquire. For the most advantageous bottom line, you need a plan. Advanced planning is concerned with two s-words: "structure" and "shelter." I am going to present the plan to you here as I present it to my clients, in four parts: (1) wealth enhancement, (2) wealth transfer, (3) wealth protection, and (4) charitable giving.

It's not enough to simply acquire wealth. You need to think ahead regarding how you can use the legal system and tax code to protect what you acquire.

1. Wealth Enhancement

Through tax-reduction strategies—business structures, tax-free dividends, tax deferral, and capital gains avoidance trusts, to name a few—along with improved cash-flow techniques, such as reducing the cost of borrowing money and lowering insurance premiums, clients can more efficiently accumulate wealth.

2. Wealth Transfer

Estate planning with trusts, life insurance, or outright gifts can maximize the transfer of wealth. Assets move tax efficiently and cost effectively, avoiding probate and any unnecessary costs. We review the current estate plan, if any, and how the assets are owned, along with beneficiary designations, and determine areas for improvement or confirm that everything is adequate as is.

3. Wealth Protection

We live in a very litigious society. Through this process we make sure clients' assets are adequately protected. We carefully review trust documents, insurance coverage, and ownership of assets, recommending further protective measures as needed. Legal structures for businesses, transferring risks to insurance companies, and other risk mitigation strategies may be recommended.

Exploring legal structures is especially important for businesses because some types of ownership can put you at risk. For instance, sole proprietors are exposed personally and are risking their own assets. If they choose to incorporate, such as filing as a C-corporation, an S-corporation, or as a limited liability company (LLC), they could protect their personal assets and also potentially reduce their income taxes, depending on the entity chosen.

The owners of S-corps and LLCs are not responsible for business liabilities. Both are legal entities created by a state filing, and both are pass-through entities, which means no income taxes are paid at the business level, and profits or losses from the business are passed through to owners' personal tax returns. Both must appoint and maintain a registered agent. They must file annual reports and pay annual fees, and they must notify the state of changes in name, registered agent, or entity type.

Those are the similarities; however, many differences exist between an S-corp and an LLC. These include ownership, ongoing formalities, management, transferability of ownership, self-employment taxes, and allocation of profits and losses. Understanding the similarities and differences is key to deciding which structure is right for you. C-corps pay a corporate tax and when profits are paid out to owners as dividends, they'll pay personal taxes on that income. Because of the liability protection, pass-through income or losses, and flexibility, LLCs appear to be the preferred entity for biotech startups. C-corps are a close second for ease of attracting investors. An entrepreneur's goals, objectives, and time horizons need to be considered before they choose a corporate structure appropriate for them and their company. Consulting a competent business attorney, CPA, and financial advisor is highly recommended.

You also need to learn about the protection offered by various types of insurance. Some of the most common include liability, IP, and employee group plans for health, life, and disability insurance, which are often part of an employee benefit package. Key person life insurance helps protect your business and cover possible lost revenue should a key employee die.

Buy-sell agreements among business partners allow those partners to purchase the other's interest in the business should one partner die. Cash value insurance allows you to use the accumulated cash value and buy out a partner's share should that partner retire or become disabled.

Insurance in qualified retirement plans may carry legal limits. Some may depend on whether you are dealing with a defined contribution or defined benefit plan.

CHARITABLE GIVING

As mentioned earlier, our goal here is to help clients who have philanthropic intent. We work on a strategy to make the biggest impact on the mission, vision, and values that are dear to them. Often clients may be interested in efforts to find treatments and cures for specific diseases because someone in their family has that disease. Others may wish to obtain a certain level of recognition for their giving, such as entry into an organization's legacy society, or funding a chair at their alma mater. Whatever a client's charitable intent is, it should be part of their advanced planning strategies, incorporating tax mitigation, asset protection, and asset transfer capabilities.

Relationship Management

Here's another equation: RM = CRM + PNRM. Relationship management (RM) *equals* client relationship management (CRM) *plus* professional network relationship management (PNRM).

CLIENT RELATIONSHIP MANAGEMENT

Without strong client relationships, an advisor's work is weakened. Our goal is to design a customized service model—including a communication style—that meets each individual client's needs most effectively. Some people want a face-to-face meeting every three or four months. Others prefer to meet only once a year. In addition to face-to-face meetings, we identify how many phone calls or online meetings a client prefers. Not everyone uses computers these days, and I need to know if someone is more comfortable without that connection. I also make sure that we are aware of which people need a phone call if the market is moving dramatically in a short period. Some appreciate being reassured over the phone. Furthermore, I try to be proactive with communicating via e-mail and social media posts.

Professional Network Relationship Management

Almost everyone can benefit from the knowledge of tax attorneys, business attorneys, CPAs, insurance specialists, and bankers. I maintain a professional network of these people, so I can analyze a case and brainstorm with them. In short, I get high-level feedback on a client's situation, without charging that client additional fees.

These experts will review our client's existing documents and plans, and we benchmark them among industry standards to make certain they are both cost effective and tax efficient. If someone is not taking advantage of certain strategies, we will determine that, and we'll bring our recommendations to the table.

For instance, some business owners could consider what are called captive insurance companies as opposed to paying commercial lines for 100 percent of their risk exposure. As I mentioned before, we have more than fifty strategies for business owners to reduce their tax liability, and they may not be taking advantage of those strategies.

Some business owner clients could be the second or third generation now running the business. However, the first or second generation still might have ownership in it. In reviewing how it is set up, we might see that the first or second generation is no longer participating in the business anymore, but their deaths will create a tax liability. To prevent or mitigate that, we can take steps today—while the first generation is still alive—from an estate-planning, asset-protection planning, and wealth-transfer point of view. Taking those immediate steps will help us get the business down to the next generation more efficiently and more cost effectively.

The Five-Step Wealth Management Consultative Process

Deciding who to trust with the task of managing your wealth is one of the most important decisions you'll ever make. Not every advisor is right for every client, nor is every client right for every advisor. This is not a business of one-size-fits-all management. We believe the best way to begin is with a complimentary discovery meeting.

1. THE DISCOVERY MEETING

The discovery meeting, the first step in our five-step process, lasts approximately ninety minutes. This meeting will determine if we can create a mutually beneficial experience for you and our firm or not. During the meeting we are going to learn a great deal about you, including your activities, hobbies, and interests. We're going to talk about your values, your goals, and the resources with which you are working. We'll cover the experiences you've had in the past with other advisors, and we'll identify who your current advisors are, and why you enjoy working with them. We want to make sure you'll derive a tremendous value in relation to the fee for our services.

This meeting will result in one of three outcomes:

1. We determine that we cannot justify our fee for the services your situation deserves. In that case we'll refer you to another advisor who may be a better fit.

2. You're doing everything quite well and there is nothing we can add to dramatically enhance your situation, so we tell you to keep doing what you're doing, and perhaps down the road we can bring your situation up to another level of sophistication.

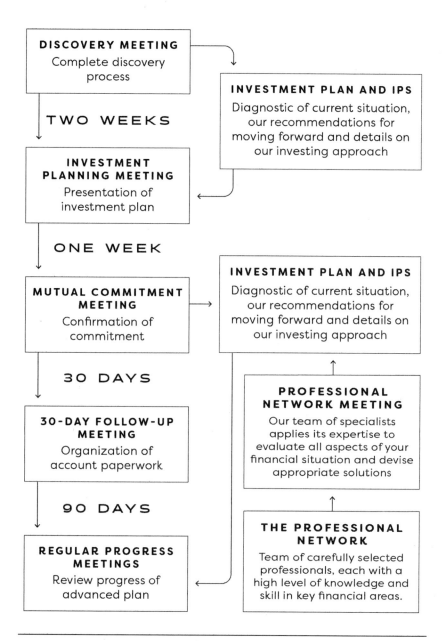

DISCOVERY MEETING
Complete discovery process

TWO WEEKS

INVESTMENT PLAN AND IPS
Diagnostic of current situation, our recommendations for moving forward and details on our investing approach

INVESTMENT PLANNING MEETING
Presentation of investment plan

ONE WEEK

MUTUAL COMMITMENT MEETING
Confirmation of commitment

INVESTMENT PLAN AND IPS
Diagnostic of current situation, our recommendations for moving forward and details on our investing approach

30 DAYS

PROFESSIONAL NETWORK MEETING
Our team of specialists applies its expertise to evaluate all aspects of your financial situation and devise appropriate solutions

30-DAY FOLLOW-UP MEETING
Organization of account paperwork

90 DAYS

THE PROFESSIONAL NETWORK
Team of carefully selected professionals, each with a high level of knowledge and skill in key financial areas.

REGULAR PROGRESS MEETINGS
Review progress of advanced plan

Graphic source: PEAK Financial Services Inc., Premier Wealth Advisors. Securities offered through Triad Advisors Member FINRA/SIPC; Advisory services offered through Peak Financial Services, Inc. Peak Financial Services, Inc. is not affiliated with Triad Advisors.

3. We determine we can add tremendous value to your situation and we welcome you to the Peak Financial "family"!

If the third outcome materializes, we'll schedule a second meeting. This is called the investment plan meeting.

2. INVESTMENT PLAN MEETING

Once we've scheduled the investment plan meeting, we research and review all the information that we've gathered during the discovery meeting. We'll establish an investment policy statement (IPS) based on the client's risk tolerance level, time constraints, and financial goals and objectives. The IPS will clarify the client's goals, provide a long-term discipline for financial decision making, and create a clear roadmap for financial success.

We'll illustrate how the existing portfolio is constructed, identify the level of risk the client is assuming, explain the existing internal fund expenses and asset management fees, and determine how tax efficient (or not) the portfolio is. We'll then identify areas for improvement in the client's investment portfolio, such as a better risk-adjusted return, a more cost-effective portfolio, and/or a more tax-efficient portfolio. We also detail our fee schedule.

At the end of that second meeting, potential clients are usually pretty certain whether they are going to move forward or not. At that point, I ask them to go home, discuss it, and if they are a couple, make sure they are both comfortable because they might want to talk about topics they wouldn't talk about with me there. We then schedule a third meeting, the mutual commitment meeting.

3. MUTUAL COMMITMENT MEETING

This takes place one or two weeks later. At this meeting we'll have all the necessary paperwork ready to open accounts with our custodian, TD Ameritrade. Transfer forms, move money authorizations, trustee certification forms, and IRA rollover forms will all be prepared as needed, and ready for the clients' review and approval. Any and all remaining questions will be answered. Once the forms are signed, we'll schedule a fourth meeting, the thirty-day follow-up meeting.

4. THIRTY-DAY FOLLOW-UP MEETING

Here, we will present your personal financial organizer. This organizer will consist of tabbed sections including the investment plan overview, your IPS, the advanced plan, account statements, and copies of all signed forms. These will also be uploaded into your encrypted, online client portal, which can be accessed 24/7. You will have already received an invitation to register on this site once your accounts are opened at TD Ameritrade. You can opt for the electronic versions of all paperwork instead of the hard copies.

Next, we'll schedule our first regular progress meeting for about two weeks out.

5. REGULAR PROGRESS MEETING

Between the mutual commitment meeting and the first regular progress meeting, we are brainstorming your advanced plan with our professional network consisting of an estate planning attorney, a CPA, an insurance specialist, and a business attorney, if needed. The advanced plan is a comprehensive evaluation of the entire range of financial needs. Specific recommendations centering around income and estate tax mitigation, risk management strategies, and asset preservation and protection concepts will come out of the professional network and be presented at the first regular progress meeting. These high-level advanced strategies are provided ancillary to our asset management fee and can be implemented with our referral sources or your existing team of professionals. However you choose to proceed, these strategies provide tremendous value and have been responsible for saving our clients hundreds of thousands, often millions, of dollars. As the advanced plan becomes implemented, quarterly, thrice-annual, or biannual progress meetings will be scheduled and performed, again, all ancillary to our assets under management fee.

Robert Toru Kiyosaki, founder of the Rich Dad Company, said, "It's not how much money you make, but how much money you keep, how hard it works for you, and how many generations you keep it for."[51]

Those are the goals I have for my clients, who've entrusted me with the job of managing their wealth. By understanding the process we adhere to, I hope you understand it's about a lot more than just managing money. It's about keeping your wealth intact!

---

51   Robert Kiyosaki, "How To See Money When Others Don't," September 24, 2013, https://www.richdad.com/Resources/Rich-Dad-Financial-Education-Blog/September-2013/how-to-see-money-when-others-don't.

Takeaway

- My definition of wealth management is threefold: wealth management *equals* investment consulting *plus* advanced planning *plus* relationship management.

- Professional network relationship management involves seeking out the advice of tax attorneys, business attorneys, CPAs, insurance specialists, and bankers with no additional charge to the client.

- More than fifty strategies for business owners to reduce their tax liability exist, and many business owners may not be taking advantage of those strategies.

- Your personality type regarding how you feel about investments and money will determine the type of advisor who is best for you.

That is how we explore and work toward meeting our clients' needs. In the next section, we are going to explore special techniques for managing wealth—including when to say *when.*

FOR
ENTREPRENEURS

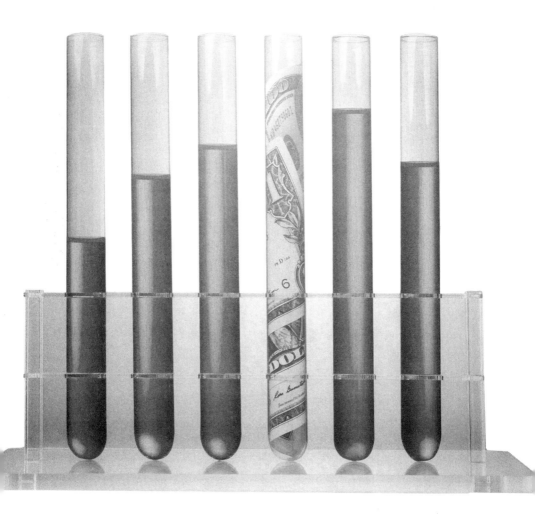

CHAPTER SIX

STARTUP AND LAUNCH: IT STARTS WITH AN IDEA

Hard working.

Creative.

Flexible.

Fearless.

Passionate.

Do you possess these traits? If so, you may have the personality to survive and even thrive in the high risk/high reward world of the biotech entrepreneur. What Investopedia calls one of the "sexiest" businesses in which to work has tremendous appeal to those excited about the potential rewards in an industry committed to fighting disease and even aging—an industry committed to improving the length and quality of human life.[52] Add that to the potential money earned in the field, and you can see why the industry continues to grow. At the beginning, and thanks to incubators, the cost seems manageable, and with a lot of long hours, hard work, and luck, your startup could be purchased by a big pharma company or go public.

Many entrepreneurs begin with a technical background, specifically scientific laboratory research. The ground floor is usually academia. Sometimes scientists involved in research for one company leave and start a new company involved in similar work.

Writing for *Life Science Network*, Leah Cannon points out that although most academics have no business training, they possess many of the traits required to be successful startup entrepreneurs. Some of the traits Cannon names are self-belief, willingness to learn, and connections.[53]

"In academia it's all about whom you know," she writes. "If you know people on grant review boards, you are more likely to

---

52   Stephen D. Simpson, "A Biotech Sector Primer," Investopedia, January 24, 2018, https://www. investopedia.com/articles/fundamental-analysis/11/primer-on-biotech-sector.asp.

53   Leah Cannon, *How to Start a Life Science Company: A Comprehensive Guide for First-Time Entrepreneurs* (Amazon Digital Services: October 2017).

get funding. If you know editors, your paper is more likely to be accepted. It is the same in the world of business. If you know a VC or two, you are more likely to get funding. If you know a crack PR firm, you are more likely to get press coverage."[54]

Six Personality Traits

Quora contributor Euwyn Poon, cofounder and president of *Spin,* named six common personality traits he has observed while collaborating with entrepreneurs:[55]

1. curiosity

2. a sense of impatience

3. sociability

4. attention to basic human needs

5. reasoning

6. flexibility

"You have to be stubborn enough to keep persevering and working on your idea, even when people tell you it's silly or you begin to doubt yourself," he writes. "But you also need to have the flexibility to recognize your first attempt may have been off the mark." He also mentions some negative adjectives such as "aggressive" and "hard-headed."[56]

Yet, those terms are really just the extreme of driven, eager, and focused. As you can see, a personality pattern emerges. Although a

---

54   Ibid.
55   Euwyn Poon, "Three Personality Traits That All Successful Entrepreneurs Share," *Forbes,* May 10, 2018, https://www.forbes.com/sites/quora/2018/05/10/three-personality-traits-that-all-successful-entrepreneurs-share/#24cac313599f.
56   Ibid.

successful biotech entrepreneur probably won't possess all these traits, she or he will no doubt exhibit some of them.

The entrepreneur must be a realist. Nothing happens in biotech without money. The initial challenge—to transition a concept into a business model—depends on the entrepreneur's ability to attract investors. From there, the journey involves developing the business, involving partners, manufacturing, and, if one is lucky, obtaining FDA approvals and regulatory requirements.

The initial challenge —to transition a concept into a business model— depends on the entrepreneur's ability to attract investors.

In seeking funding, entrepreneurs need to understand—and describe—the market they will be serving. Having a clear understanding of only the technical aspects isn't enough. As is the case in any startup, regardless of the industry, finding the right people is crucial. Occasionally an entrepreneur is able to handle both administrative and technical sides of the business, but in most cases, hiring someone with top administrative skills increases a business's chances of success.

Before his death in 2014, Stan Yakatan founded or cofounded more than twenty companies in the US, Canada, Israel, France, the Netherlands, Poland, Australia, Taiwan, and Germany, and in his fifty-year career, he often served as CEO and chairman.

In a 2010 *Life Science Leader* interview with Karl Schmieder, Yakatan and two other biotech entrepreneurs discussed, among other topics, what led them to the field, challenges facing the industry, and what it takes to succeed.

Yakatan said he learned with his first job that he wasn't willing to play politics. His second position offered him independence, although he admitted he knew nothing about "raising money or valuations."[57]

When asked how he chose the particular area in which he started his company, Yakatan said, "I had, and still have, one rule: Meet unmet medical needs. There is a significant difference between innovation and commercialization, although most people put them together. Very few companies are started on innovation alone. A lot of people take existing ideas and try to make them better, but few people make new ideas. I look for the new ideas."[58]

Yet MEBO International CEO Kevin Xu advises that creating a new biotech product that provides incremental improvements to existing solutions is easier and less expensive than creating an entirely new category.

"Everything from regulatory approval to marketing becomes simpler if you have a listed product, a benchmark or an equivalent technology to compare to yours," Xu says in a *Forbes* article.[59]

Biotech pioneer and Nobel Laureate Walter Gilbert, whom I discussed earlier in this book, told me that, from an early age, he knew he would be a scientist:

"The people in my generation who went into science did not go into science for monetary reasons," he said. "In fact, they never even thought of the monetary connection … The whole fixation on what do I do, how do I get a job, what is my career path going to be—well, it wasn't there. It wasn't a question one phrased."

---

57   Karl Schmieder, "What Does It Take to Succeed As a Bioentrepreneur?" *Life Science Leader,* September 15, 2010, https://www.pharmaceuticalonline.com/doc/what-does-it-take-to-succeed-as-a-0001.
58   Ibid.
59   Kevin Xu, "Five Things You Must Know to Make Your Startup Successful," *Forbes,* July 14, 2014, https://www.forbes.com/sites/theyec/2014/07/14/five-things-you-must-know-to-make-your-startup-successful-in-biotech/#77174173309d.

Now, of course, through necessity, anyone considering a career in biotech must question and explore what that career path is and where it leads.

Now, for the Business.

We've just looked at some of the personal traits of successful startup entrepreneurs, but what about the startup itself? Writing for *Quora,* entrepreneur and molecular biologist Scott R. Sacane names location, venture capital, partners, and size as important factors to a startup's success. As already stated in this book, he points out that most successful startups are located in Boston, San Francisco, or San Jose. As for venture capitalists, he says that large, established VCs are able to provide the necessary capital to navigate the high risk, along with the necessary connections to make introductions to potential partners.[60]

Although the majority of successful companies will have partnerships, Sacane points out, they are not essential in the startup stage. Size matters, but only when it comes to money. "Past successes were characterized more by diversity of founding teams than head count ..." he says. "In an industry like biotechnology where capital requirements are high, timelines are long and high rates of failure is the norm, cash is king and past successes almost always remained well capitalized during their early years."[61]

---

60 "What Are the Characteristics of the Top Biotech Startups?" Quora, June 28, 2012, https://www.quora.com/What-are-the-characteristics-of-the-top-biotech-startups.

61 Ibid.

Three People Plus Grants Equals Startup

A startup doesn't have to be massive to make its mark. Walter Gilbert told me about a small biotech company—staffed by only three people—that is doing a 130-person Phase 2 trial in ALS at twenty-six sites around the country. The two principals came up with the idea for the company when they were undergraduate students at Brown.

"They saved up some money, and they started a company," Gilbert told me. "[They] took jobs as lab technicians, saved a little money, have gotten large grants, and now they've raised about $10 million and are doing this large ALS trial combination of drugs ... It's fun. I love small companies, but some of that is the different world we are in now" versus when Gilbert started. "The investment world is wildly different."

Location, Location, Location

If you are located in a biotech hub, you will have the benefit of community. Top universities, successful entrepreneurs in your field, lab space, and local venture capital will be available. The ripples we discussed earlier in this book reach farther and involve more people and products in a biotech hub. Take Kendall Square. Densely populated and fast moving, the Cambridge area offers an entrepreneur more than 120 biotech firms, in addition to suppliers, patent attorneys, and contract research organizations. Hubs also offer numerous networking opportunities. Boston's MassBio is an important one.

Overall, it's safe to say you will have more opportunities working in a hub. You'll also have more competition for investors and attention.

Rewards

In addition to the satisfaction inherent in such work, financial rewards can be high.

"Biotechnology entrepreneurs may draw initial salaries of $150,000 or more and can potentially claim very valuable options should their startup companies eventually go public. A number of CEOs ultimately became multimillionaires on the strength of such options in the biotech boom of the late 1990s."[62]

The total global biotech market was estimated at $415 billion in 2017.[63]

Challenges Entrepreneurs Face

Although passion is the fuel that drives most startups, entrepreneurs soon learn they will have to navigate many bumps along the way. In writing this book, many people spoke candidly with me about their challenges and how they did or didn't overcome them.

One of the biggest mistakes, they said, concerns money. The message here is if you don't have the funding for your startup, still start it up.

> *The message here is if you don't have the funding for your startup, still start it up.*

"Use whatever money you have to do whatever you can to move your R&D program forward. If you can't afford lab space or equipment yet, outsource some

---

62   Encyclopedia.com, "Biotechnology Entrepreneur," January 28, 2019, https://www.encyclopedia.com/medicine/medical-magazines/biotechnology-entrepreneur.

63   Transparency Market Research, "Global Biotechnology Market by Application (Biopharmacy, Bioservices, Bioagri, Bioindustrial), by Technology (Fermentation, Tissue Regeneration, PCR, Nanobiotechnology, DNA Sequencing & Others) - Industry Analysis, Size, Share, Growth, Trends and Forecast, 2010 – 2017," April 2013, https://www.transparencymarketresearch.com/biotechnology-market.html.

experiments where you can. Do all of this right now. Do whatever you can to generate value in your company. If you have savings, use them to build your startup. Borrow money if you are able to, especially if you are able to access low-interest credit. Lend your startup money. Do whatever you can to raise cash to invest in your company. If you are to be successful, investors want to see you have 'skin in the game'; you have to be willing to take on risk in your startup if you ever want someone else to."[64]

Another major challenge is deciding which person on the team is going to make the business decisions. The CEO should be that person. Your CEO must be focused on business and only that.

Failing to empower the executive team can also destroy your startup. Even the founders must step back and let those who are involved in the business decide what is best for the business.

Refusing to network, especially when you're busy with a project, might seem like the most sensible path, but if you follow that instinct, you can cut off an important lifeline for your business.

In the *Life Science Leader* interview, Yakatan talks about the mistakes he sees being made by first-time entrepreneurs, and the first one he names is their belief that technology is all important:

"It's cliché, but you can have the best technology and the worst management team, and the company will fail. You can have the worst technology and the best management team, and the company will succeed. Management is more important than technology."[65] Second, he says entrepreneurs should beware of the trends.

"Hot markets are risky. There are at least twenty-five companies in the RNAi space right now, and few of them will succeed," he

---

64   Lab Launch Blog, "The 8 Mistakes (Almost) Every Biotech Startup Makes," August 9, 2016, https://lablaunchblog.wordpress.com/2016/08/09/the-8-mistakes-almost-every-biotech-startup-makes/.

65   Schmieder, op. cit.

says. "It was the same thing with monoclonals, with combinatorial chemistry, with every new platform. How many companies have failed in each of those spaces?"[66]

He sums up his tips by emphasizing the importance of good communication and taking the time to be sure that others understand your concepts. It's critical. Finally, he warns not to rely too much on advice given to you by investors and attorneys.

"Very few VCs and even fewer attorneys have in-house, company-building experience," he says. "You need to create synergy between founders, advisors, and investors, and challenge any of them if they threaten your vision."[67]

As you deal with the day-to-day challenges and obstacles, you are preparing for the ultimate challenge of the FDA. Federal oversight of biotechnology originated in the 1970s when NIH published a set of research guidelines in response to concerns raised by scientists engaged in recombinant DNA research. As mentioned earlier in this book, many an entrepreneur has made it through all the steps to bring a product to market only to fail to win FDA approval.

"The FDA is actually a good model, and the FDA for small companies is totally eager to help launch things," Gilbert told me. "But entrepreneurs come out of business school, and if they listen to big pharma, they've heard all the wrong things, and their political attitude is very often that they should not be willing to listen to government."

Gilbert acknowledged that, every now and then, one might encounter an individual in the FDA who is "a real pain and does strange things."

---

66   Ibid.
67   Ibid.

DRUG DEVELOPMENT

Discovery & Preclinical	Phase I	Phase II	Phase III	NDA/BLA

PROBABILITY OF

Phase Success:	66%	32%	61%	86%
Approval	**11%**	**17%**	**52%**	**86%**

COMPOUNDS NEEDED

to reach approval:	10	5	2	1

Source: David W. Thomas, John L. Craighead, Celia Economides, and Jesse Rosenthal, "Clinical Development Success Rates for Investigational Drugs," Nature Biotechnology, January 9, 2014, https://www.nature.com/articles/nbt.2786.

For example, Gilbert recalled being involved in a company that was trying to develop drugs to enhance memory.

"The guy from the FDA at that time did not believe that such drugs could exist—or should exist—so he was not going to approve any trials. Question: 'Can I get a drug to enhance memory?' Well, he thinks it's all you know."

However, overall, Gilbert said, "the FDA is fairly reasonable—helpful but also demanding."

Planning for Success

So, what does it take for a company to be successful? According to Yakatan, "A four-letter word: luck. Well, two words, luck and management. The ability to start a successful company and launch a drug requires luck and great management."[68]

Ultimately, every biotech entrepreneur is like every other entrepreneur, regardless of the field. You have an idea you believe in, and you are going to focus all your efforts, talent, and money on making it become a reality. As stated earlier, in the biotech industry, even if you fail, you win because the experience you gained will only help you move on with your career.

I've intended this chapter to be both honest and positive. Yes, entrepreneurs lose fortunes and hope in biotech, but they do that in other industries as well. Perhaps because I have been involved with clients in the industry and because I live and work in one of the geographical centers of the boom, I am passionate about biotech as a career and an investment. What other career field could offer such great rewards as well as the potential to affect, help, and heal our current and future populations in such a major way?

---

68   Ibid.

Takeaway

- In obtaining funding, you should be able to understand—and describe—the market you will serve.

- In most cases, hiring someone with top administrative skills increases a business's chances of success.

- A startup doesn't have to be massive.

- Biotech hubs offer more competition but more advantages and a sense of community.

- Challenges include raising money. But even if you don't have the funding, you can still start.

- Management is as important as technology.

- Remember that networking is a key lifeline for your business.

- In the biotech industry, even if you fail, you win.

CHAPTER SEVEN

POSTLAUNCH WEALTH-BUILDING STRATEGIES

Building a biotech company is more than a job; it's a lifestyle. As you build that company, it's easy to overlook the fact that you must also be building your wealth. Many of our clients come to us with concentrated positions in the form of common stock, restricted stock, restricted stock units, and/or stock options from companies they're currently with or ones they have recently left. Some are worried about market risk, or want to know about divesting strategies, while others are seeking tax-reduction strategies. Often clients need guidance in all three areas. As is the case with everything else that matters in life, you need a plan—one that is not one-size-fits-all. It is called wealth management, and it organizes all facets of your financial life to give you an overall structure geared toward your needs. This chapter will introduce you to unique strategies for business owners that others can't take advantage of—strategies to reduce taxes and accumulate wealth. Some are well known, while others are less known and understood.

Keeping What You Make

You don't need me to tell you that business owners don't always pay themselves first. They put their money into the business. However, you can't put all your money back in and hope to sell the business one day. Again, you need to manage your wealth, starting now.

"Wealth management is simply the art and science of solving financial and related problems and concerns to enhance your personal financial situation," writes Russ Alan Prince and John J. Bowen Jr. in their book, *Becoming Seriously Wealthy.* "It is designed to address the full range of your personal wealth challenges on an ongoing, long-term basis, in a way that coordinates all the disparate aspects of your wealth. It is holistic and synergistic, thereby enabling you to leverage your wealth and even your business to increase the probability that you will become seriously wealthy."[69]

Rapidly Accumulated Wealth, and Then What?

The biotech industry is one where hard-working, talented individuals can—with some luck—accumulate great wealth in a relatively short period of time. It then becomes the job of a team of advisors—a financial advisor, a CPA, an estate planning attorney, and a business attorney—to show the client how to hang onto and build upon that wealth.

That's what my firm does. We collaborate as a team of experts in various fields to provide advice that is both financially sound and legal. In chapter 5, we discussed that wealth management is investment consulting *plus* advanced planning *plus* relationship management, and we pointed out that true wealth management goes far beyond advising you on investments. You may need more than investment advice. You may be looking for ways to protect your wealth or reduce taxes—probably both.

Tax Reduction Strategies

Let's look at tax reduction. Of course, you write off the expenses you can legally use against your business. You probably max out your contributions to a 401(k), and you may even have after-tax accounts invested in tax-free municipal bonds.

---

69   Russ Alan Prince and John J. Bowen, *Becoming Seriously Wealthy: How to Harness the Strategies of the Super Rich and Ultra-Wealthy Business Owners,* (San Martin, California: AES Nation, 2017).

In addition to the aforementioned traditional tax-reduction strategies, business owners should also consider advanced wealth accumulation vehicles, such as nonqualified deferred compensation plans, defined-benefit pension plans, captive insurance companies, private placement life insurance, and private placement variable annuities.

QUALIFIED RETIREMENT PLANS: WHAT ARE THE BENEFITS?

Qualified retirement plans are legal ways to shelter assets from taxes. You pay taxes only when the funds are withdrawn. Employers and employees alike can contribute portions of their salary to their qualified retirement plans. As soon as you start to generate significant cash flow, you should be seriously considering your retirement plan options—or you risk paying too much in taxes.

There are two categories of qualified plans: defined contribution plans and defined benefit plans.

With a defined contribution plan, such as a 401(k), owners and employees contribute on their own behalf from their salary. Contributions are made on a pretax basis and are not taxed until taken out. Employers can match employee contributions, and they receive a tax deduction for the matching amounts. Investments in mutual funds, stock, or ETFs are most common in these plans.

Defined benefit plan participants are promised a percentage of their compensation to be received at retirement. If appropriate, business owners can enjoy larger contributions than other qualified plans, greater tax deductions, tax-deferred growth, an ability to receive a substantial share of the plan assets for themselves, and possibly more predictable benefits in retirement.

As you can see, these are great tax-saving options—and there are more.

NONQUALIFIED DEFERRED COMPENSATION PLANS

Nonqualified retirement plans offer individuals added tax benefits on top of their regular retirement plans. There is no tax deduction for employer contributions, but executives' pretax wages are deducted from their paychecks at their discretion. The plan's contributions and earnings grow tax-deferred until the executive withdraws them, usually upon retiring. These plans can be very attractive to highly compensated executives and can be used to complement vesting schedules of restricted stock, RSUs, and the exercising of stock options to soften the tax hit in the same year.

Advantages and Disadvantages

Nonqualified plans have several advantages over their qualified counterparts:

- *No limits on contributions.* Hundreds of thousands of dollars may be placed in these plans at the discretion of the employer or employee in a single year.

- *Tax-deferred growth.* As long as the segregation and forfeiture requirements are satisfied, all money placed inside these plans grows tax-deferred just as it would in an IRA or other qualified plan.

- *Insurance benefits.* If life insurance is used in a nonqualified plan, it can pay substantial death benefits. Furthermore, modern policies can provide several different types of protection in a single policy with the use of riders that pay out benefits for disability, critical illness, and long-term care, in addition to death. This type of policy effectively provides the employee with a package of benefits that he or she can count on as long as the terms of the plan are met.

- *Freedom from ERISA regulations.* Nonqualified plans are not beholden to ERISA regulations that prohibit discrimination among employees and require top-heavy testing for qualified retirement plans. Therefore, certain classes of employees can be singled out to gain access to the nonqualified plan.

- *Substantial flexibility.* Nonqualified plans can be structured many different ways according to the needs of the participants.

- *Additional advantages.* These plans require minimal reporting and filing and are usually cheaper to establish and maintain than qualified plans.

Some of the limitations of nonqualified plans include substantial risk of forfeiture. Funds placed in nonqualified plans are usually subject to attachment from creditors—unlike money in qualified plans. If this is not the case, the plan could become null and void, and the employee could be responsible for paying taxes on all the funds within the plan. In short, the money in these plans is not unconditionally available to the employee, and if it is, it will be considered income, and thus taxable.

CAPTIVE INSURANCE COMPANIES

Another way companies are reducing overhead costs and increasing owners' profitability is through the use of captive insurance companies, better known as captives. According to R. Wesley Sierk, III, "Captives offer unparalleled benefits for the companies that use them. They allow a company to obtain insurance coverage that is tailored to its unique risks, rather than the standard coverages provided in commercial policies. Captives also allow a company's risk to be judged on its own merit, rather than being charged a premium that is based on the risks of its entire industry. Captives also provide tax benefits for the companies who use them and often provide claims handling services that are substantially better than the service provided by commercial insurers."[70]

A feasibility test can determine if a captive is right for your company. Existing coverages, premiums, cash reserves, claims history, and unique risks are all taken into consideration. If appropriate, a proposal is presented that details potential premium savings, tax savings, and future profitability projections. Many businesses are profiting tremendously from these plans as opposed to paying premiums to commercial insurance companies.

PRIVATE PLACEMENT LIFE INSURANCE AND PRIVATE PLACEMENT ANNUITIES

Now, I know what you're thinking: life insurance and annuities—really? However, we're not talking about the traditional retail policies for most people. The two words "private placement" should begin to distinguish these plans from the everyday, retail contracts anyone can buy. These plans are specifically designed to accommodate large

---

70 R. Wesley Sierk, III, *Taken Captive* (RMA Press: February 2008).

lump sums of money—$500,000 and up. Because of these large allocations, the costs compared to retail plans are dramatically lower. These plans take advantage of the tax code surrounding life insurance and annuities, such as tax-deferred growth. For life insurance, added benefits include tax-free withdrawals while you are alive, and tax-free death benefits to heirs. With the use of charitable planning tools, such as private foundations and donor advised funds, the tax-free transfer of wealth to the next generation using these policies can be dramatically enhanced.

According to Prince and Bowen, the super-rich are strongly gravitating toward private placement life insurance and private placement variable annuities because they don't believe that taxes on investments are going to be cut appreciably in the future, and "the effects of tax-free compounding on their investment returns can be astounding."[71]

When you think about your accumulated wealth, it is important to pay attention to how much you will have, not just after you earn it, but after taxes. That's where private placement life insurance and private placement annuities come in.

Basic life insurance includes term and permanent policies. Usually geared toward young families, term policies are inexpensive

> **When you think about your accumulated wealth, it is important to pay attention to how much you will have, not just after you earn it, but after taxes.**

in the early years and provide only a death benefit. As the name implies, they are in place for a set term, and then they expire or become cost-prohibitive to continue. Permanent life insurance policies build cash value over time, and provide a death benefit that could be paid up and permanent. These policies could

---

71   Russ Alan Prince and John J. Bowen, op. cit.

either be whole life or universal life insurance. It can take years to see your cash value equal or exceed the amount of premiums you've paid, often ten to fifteen years or more. These are great for individuals in their thirties and forties with established cash flow who can accumulate in them for twenty years or more.

Private placement life insurance, when set up properly, can provide both estate protection for your heirs and also tax-free accumulation of wealth. Private placement life insurance (also known as PPLI) is a customized version of variable life insurance. If you haven't heard about it, that's because this insurance is not available to the general public. Most private placement life insurance policies are offered by banks, hedge fund managers, and niche insurance companies. These policies are usually only offered to accredited or qualified investors who meet certain net worth and income levels, along with investment experience.

With all cash value life insurance, the following tax benefits are:

- *Tax-deferred growth.* The cash value of the policy can increase, tax-deferred.

- *No K-1 tax reporting.* Investment returns inside PPLI and PPVAs are not reported on K-1s like hedge fund investment returns.

- *Tax-free access.* Although loans and withdrawals can reduce the death benefit of the policy, access to accumulated cash value by way of loans or withdrawals is tax-free.

- *Tax-free passing along to heirs.* PPLI will transfer to heirs tax-free at the insured's death. If held in a life insurance trust, it will also avoid estate taxes.

Compare the taxes you could pay on the profits from a taxable investment (as much as 49 percent in Massachusetts for federal and state taxes) to what initially may look like great returns on that investment. Now, consider that the private placement life insurance and private placements annuities allow you to avoid taxes on those returns.

In addition to the tax benefits of life insurance, PPLI offers those who qualify for it, low institutional pricing, low commissions and fees compared to publicly offered policies, and a wider array of investment choices and strategies.

CASE STUDY: PPLI[72]

Let's look at an example. John Jones is a successful businessman with $50 million of investable assets. John loves his hedge fund investments but realizes more than half of his 2013 profits will benefit the federal and state governments. To compare the benefits of PPLI, he asks his agent to illustrate a $10 million single premium PPLI policy and compare it to a $10 million taxable hedge fund investment (see Figure below).

PPLI vs. Hedge Fund Returns				
Age	Investment	PPLI End-Of-Year Cash Value	Death Benefit (Including Cash Value)	Hedge Fund Taxable (53% Tax)
50	$10,000,000	$10,583,149	$41,162,000	$10,376,000
55		13,862,975	41,162,000	12,026,792
60		19,365,400	41,162,000	14,464,374
70		39,085,869	45,339,608	20,921,810
80		80,302,482	84,317,606	30,262,088
90		163,260,398	171,423,418	43,772,215

Assuming there is a net annual 8 percent return, PPLI generates $4.9 million more than a taxable hedge fund investment after 10 years. After twenty years, PPLI has outperformed by over $18 million.

---

72   Edward A. Renn, "Keeping What You Make," PrivateWealth.com, March 7, 2013, https://www.fa-mag.com/news/keeping-what-you-make-13577.html.

Held for forty years, the PPLI policy will produce $120 million more than a taxable account. The outperformance will only increase if the investment returns are higher. And, should tax rates increase, this could also help the PPLI product out-perform.

Private Placement Variable Annuity

A private placement variable annuity (PPVA) enables you to defer income taxes on the growth of your portfolios within the annuity structure. Like private placement life insurance, it has similar tax advantages, and it may be easier to obtain.

Some prefer to make a not-for-profit, such as a private foundation, the beneficiary of a private placement variable annuity. Doing so allows all the deferred investment gains to remain tax free when the owner dies.

As is the case with most tax-deferred annuities, with PPVAs you need to realize that the gains on any funds taken out of the annuity while you're alive are considered income and taxed accordingly. Furthermore, until you are fifty-nine and a half years old, you must pay a 10 percent excise tax on deferred investment gains if you withdraw them.

Wealth-Protection Strategies

BASIC ESTATE PLANNING FOR BUSINESS OWNERS

The foundational documents for most estates of means, especially business owners', begin with an up-to-date will, health-care proxy (for Massachusetts residents), living will (for other state residencies), durable powers of attorney, and a living revocable trust.

The will is a document that spells out your wishes regarding how your assets should be distributed in the event of your death. If you die without a will, it is called "dying intestate." The state would then direct how and to whom your assets are to be transferred, which may go against your wishes. You can name the person you want to settle your estate, called the executor. You can also name a guardian for minor children or dependents with special needs. Again, if you do not name anyone, the state can appoint someone who you may not want to carry out these duties. The tradeoff to transferring assets through a will is that it is a public record and must be probated. This means the will is settled through the probate court system, and in many states that can be a long, arduous process.

In Massachusetts, a health-care proxy spells out your advance medical directives. Some states refer to this document as a living will. This lets others know what you want in the event you are incapacitated and can't make medical decisions on your own. Without this document, medical care providers must prolong your life using artificial means. This might keep you artificially alive well beyond your family's financial means to do so.

A durable power of attorney document appoints someone to make financial and legal decisions for you in the event you are unable to do so on your own. While not exhaustive, this document allows the appointee to do things like pay your bills, make investment decisions, file your taxes, or change ownership and beneficiaries. This person must be someone you explicitly trust to do the right thing for your benefit.

Your final basic estate planning document is called a living revocable trust. Your assets are placed into the trust while you're alive, and the trust then supersedes your will, allowing transfer of your assets without probate when you die. A trust will not protect your assets from creditors or ex-spouses, however.

ADVANCED ESTATE PLANNING

For your estate to be taxed at the federal level, in 2018, it needs to be over $11.2 million, although your spouse can inherit an unlimited amount from your estate without estate taxes via the unlimited marital deduction. If the spouse inherits the estate, after their own death, the succeeding heirs might have a federal estate tax problem. At the state tax level, the exemption amount for estates in Massachusetts is $1 million, and an unlimited marital deduction is also in effect. But if your estate exceeds $1 million, and you forego the use of your exemption amounts and pass everything to your spouse, you're just postponing the inevitable taxes on the estate. By use of an exemption equivalent trust, decedents can take advantage of these exclusion amounts at the first death, and have the remaining amounts go via the unlimited marital deduction. The trust value can then grow to an unlimited amount and still avoid estate taxes upon the second person's death.

BUSINESS VALUE "FREEZE" TECHNIQUE

If you want to maximize your wealth and transfer more to your heirs someday, an estate "freeze" on the value of your business can be very effective. Essentially, from the point in time in which you establish the freeze, any appreciation on the value of the frozen amount of your business can pass to your heirs free from estate taxes. This strategy is implemented using a certain type of trust that transfers closely-held stock, at a discount, into the trust. The trust can then purchase more shares, again at a discount, from the grantor (the business owner). Depending on the business valuation, this can potentially save the next generation several million dollars.

PREMIUM-FINANCED LIFE INSURANCE

As the term implies, premiums are financed to open and keep the policy in force. This strategy allows the policy owner to save a substantial amount of money compared to paying the premiums from their own cash or cash flow. The borrower may pay interest only for a set period of time, such as five years. The cash value and death benefit can be collateralized for the lender and can ultimately be used to help pay the loan off if structured properly. To avoid and help pay for estate taxes, an irrevocable life insurance trust (ILIT) can own the policy. If established this way, proceeds will be income and estate tax-free.

Premium financing is used for large death benefits and can be established for estate liquidity, business purposes like "key person" insurance, or funding a shareholder's agreement.

There you have some intriguing strategies to consider, and we haven't even touched on important topics such as liquidity events. We will do that, though—in the next chapter.

Takeaway

- Set up properly, a private placement life insurance policy can provide both estate protection for your heirs and tax-free growth of wealth. As a rule, fees and commissions are lower than for publicly offered policies.

- A private placement variable annuity, somewhat similar to private placement life insurance, has similar tax-deferred growth advantages, and it may be easier to obtain.

- There are two types of qualified plans: defined contribution plans, such as 401(k)s, and defined benefit plans, which allow much larger tax deductions and more predictable retirement income.

- Deferred compensation plans are the most common of the nonqualified plans. They allow highly paid executives to defer more money pretax than a qualified plan, such as a 401(k).

CHAPTER EIGHT

PLANNING FOR LIQUIDITY EVENTS

Question: When do the founders, investors, and employees receive cash from their equity holdings? Answer: Usually, when a liquidity event occurs. If a private company, instead of paying out dividends, has reinvested cash flow in the business, the liquidity event will be the first time shareholders receive a significant return on their investment.

> A liquidity event is an event that allows founders and early investors in a company to cash out some or all of their ownership shares. The liquidity event is considered an exit strategy for an illiquid investment—that is, for equity that has little or no market to trade on. Founders of a firm, naturally, drive toward a liquidity event, and its investors along the way—venture capital firms, angel investors or private equity firms—hope for or expect one within a reasonable amount of time after initially making an investment.[73]

Types of Liquidity Events

Licensing. Merger. Acquisition. Public offering. All of these can and do occur in the biotech industry. The most common liquidity events occur when a company goes public with an initial public offering (IPO) or gets acquired by another company. At that time, those owners and venture capital firms who provided seed or early round investments—along with early employees of the company—are able to cash in. Founders of the firm may or may not be interested in a liquidity event. When a firm is acquired, an initial liquidity event is

---

73   "Liquidity Event," Investopedia, last updated January 30, 2018, accessed January 2019, https://www.investopedia.com/terms/l/liquidity_event.asp.

followed with potentially more compensation as the founders and employees work out terms with the new owners.

As of this writing, one of biotech's largest "unicorns" (a privately held startup company valued at over $1 billion), Cambridge-based Moderna Therapeutics, is planning to go public with an IPO of as much as $500 million. That makes it among the largest ever IPOs in Massachusetts for any type of company. Moderna was recently valued at more than $7 billion—and the boom ripples on!

Taxes

As the term implies, a "liquidity event" turns illiquid private stock into liquid and tradeable shares of public company stock, or in an all-cash transaction, fully liquid cash. When this event occurs, it usually creates a taxable event for the shareholders being bought out. Therefore, anticipating the tax liability associated with the event is paramount, and needs to be planned for accordingly.

It's likely you understand there's a difference between the terms "tax avoidance" and "tax evasion." Tax avoidance is using the letter of the law to mitigate the tax consequences of a taxable event, such as an IPO. Tax evasion is an unlawful attempt to circumvent the payment of taxes due as the result of a taxable event. There are many lawful and effective strategies to utilize in reducing one's tax liability. You can rest assured we'll be focused on the legal ones throughout this book.

Types of stocks you may hold prior to the liquidity event include the following:

- common stock
- convertible debt

- restricted stock and restricted stock units (RSUs)

- qualified small business stock (QSBS)

- nonqualified (NQ) and incentive stock options (ISOs)

These are all forms of equity incentive compensation, which most founders, directors, and executives may hold. The difference between what the shareholder has paid for the shares and the price at which the shares are sold is called a "capital gain." The length of time the shares have been held determines if it is a short or long-term capital gain. With shares held for less than twelve months, it will be considered a short-term capital gain and subject to the shareholder's ordinary income tax. In 2018, that can be up to 37 percent federal and 5.1 percent state (in Massachusetts) tax, or a total of 42.1 percent. Capital gains on shares held longer than twelve months are subject to long-term capital gain taxes of up to 23.8 percent federal (20 percent long-term capital gains plus 3.8 percent Medicare surcharge tax) and 5.1 percent in Massachusetts, for a total of 28.9 percent. Given that millions of dollars may be at stake, it's imperative that shareholders anticipate the tax consequences of a liquidity event, and understand all the legal tax-mitigation strategies at their disposal ahead of time. We will examine these further in chapter 11.

Pre-IPO

The illiquid nature of privately held stock has its own unique risks. Aileen Lee of Cowboy Ventures found that only .14 percent (fourteen out of one thousand) startup tech companies meet the definition of a unicorn.[74] Therefore, the journey from startup to a successful liquidity

---

74   Aileen Lee and Ted Wang, "Announcing Cowboy Ventures III, a $95m Fund to Back Seed-Stage Tech Ventures," Cowboy Ventures, August 7, 2018, https://cowboy.vc/blog/?author=3.

event can be long, arduous, and many times not very profitable. Also, the strategies for managing nonpublic stock can be more complex than public company stock as well. Employees should understand what could happen to the value of their stock options or restricted shares before a company goes public or gets bought through a merger or acquisition. The term "dilution" should be fully understood as people sign on to a start-up. Venture capital (VC)-backed start-ups will generally need multiple rounds of financing. Every time a new round occurs, the original shareholders' share value gets reduced, or diluted, because new shares of the company get issued on each subsequent round. Preferably, in the end, you'll own a smaller percentage of a larger whole.

Also, when VCs buy stock in a private company, they do not buy common stock, which is the class of stock you receive from your option exercise. Instead, they universally buy what's called "convertible preferred stock." A liquidation preference is an essential element of convertible preferred stock. This preference means that, when the company is sold, the venture capital investors are given a choice: (1) either they can take the sale proceeds (cash and/or stock) "off the top" and get their investment back together with a specified dividend (like interest) that has been accumulating; or (2) they can convert to common stock and get what the common stockholders get.

Senior executives may protect themselves, along with competent lawyers, by negotiating contracts with performance-based incentives, dilution protective devices, "Make Whole" contractual guarantees, and cash incentive payments. In order to be effective, these strategies should be discussed with your attorney and put in writing before signing onto a start-up.

IPOs Are Unique

With all initial public offerings (IPOs), investors, including VC firms, convert their preferred stock to common stock before the shares trade publicly. This can sometimes give employees a better financial reward and outcome than a merger or acquisition. Before the IPO, a selling price must be determined, and in order for the shares to equal the selling price, either a "reverse-split" or "forward-split" may occur. This doesn't mean your share value gets diluted or increased, it just means you'll need to wait until this occurs to accurately value your total holdings.

Post-IPO and Lock-Ups

After a stock debuts on the publicly traded stock markets, founders, directors, executives, and early institutional investors usually face a "lockup period" when they're prohibited from selling their shares, typically six months from the IPO date. After that, these original shareholders may sell their shares. However, if they are restricted or control securities, SEC Rule 144 will need to be complied with.

According to the SEC, "Restricted securities are securities acquired in unregistered, private sales from the issuing company or from an affiliate of the issuer. Investors typically receive restricted securities through private placement offerings, Regulation D offerings, employee stock benefit plans, as compensation for professional services, or in exchange for providing 'seed money' or startup capital to the company ... Control securities are those held by an affiliate of the issuing company."[75]

---

75   "Rule 144: Selling Restricted and Control Securities," US Securities and Exchange Commission, updated January 16, 2013, accessed January 2019, https://www.sec.gov/reportspubs/investor-publications/investorpubsrule144htm.html.

To avoid impacting the selling price of the securities, sales should take place in a methodical, measured pace. For large transactions, it's not uncommon to negotiate lower sales prices and even have transaction fees waived if the proceeds will be managed with the same brokerage firm.

Tax Implications

After the company goes public, you face risks during the lockup period when the stock cannot be immediately sold. If the stock is instead sold at the end of the 180-day lockup, you can actually lose money. Your tax is payable at ordinary income tax rates (applied to the difference between the stock market price at the time of exercise over the price paid), which can exceed your gain if the stock price falls far enough. There is also the alternative minimum tax, which complicates the actual tax consequences for ISOs.

You should always make sure you have enough liquid cash available to pay the taxes that will become due, generally within two weeks of the same calendar quarter as when the IPO occurred.

You should always make sure you have enough liquid cash available to pay the taxes that will become due, generally within two weeks of the same calendar quarter as when the IPO occurred. Planning with your wealth management advisory team before this event occurs is critical!

Complying with Securities Laws

Senior officers and directors of public companies must comply with five important areas before selling shares of company stock. They are covered under general securities laws, the Sarbanes-Oxley Act of 2002, and the Dodd-Frank Wall Street Reform and Consumer Protection Act of 2010. They are as follows:

1. notice and reporting

2. controlled sales of "founder stock"

3. no trading on material, nonpublic information

4. no "short-swing" profits for corporate insiders

5. no favorable financing for senior executives

Large and influential shareholders must notify the market of their intent to sell shares of their company stock ahead of time. They must disclose the volume and who the selling party is. Changes in shareholder ownership must be updated after the sale takes place as well. The corporation must approve the intended sale and keep the SEC informed of the changes. To satisfy Sarbanes-Oxley, these transactions must be reported on SEC Form 4 by the end of the second day following the date of the transaction.

Controlled sales of "founder stock" are governed by SEC Rules 144 and 145. Founders and executives who acquired company stock other than on the open market, must follow strict rules governing disposition of such shares. Rules around the holding period, public information, trading volumes, types of transactions permitted, and filing notices must all be adhered to and executed correctly.

Trading on material, nonpublic information is considered insider trading and is illegal, and can be met with fines and possible jail time. SEC Rule 10b-5 specifies that no one may legally buy or sell stock based on important information not available to the general public. We all can recall how unlikely it seemed that Martha Stewart, America's homemaker, would ever go to jail, but this is the exact reason for her incarceration in 2004.

Insiders—anyone who is an officer, director, or holder of more than 10 percent of the company's shares—are not allowed to keep profits made from the purchase and sale of company stock if both transactions occur within six months of each other, otherwise known as "short-swing" profits.

Insider loans are another no-no. In a 2002 *New York Times* article on the practice—once followed by the likes of Gap, Compaq Computer, and Home Depot—David Leonhardt wrote, "No bank would make loans like these. One is for $2 million, to be repaid over five years with no interest. Two others, one for $5 million and one for $10 million, will be forgiven if the borrowers keep their current jobs for a few years."[76] Under Sarbanes-Oxley, these types of loans to public company corporate insiders are now prohibited.

As you can see, navigating and adhering to these rules can be tricky stuff. Any planned and pending dispositions of company stock by insiders should be discussed with their corporate counsel and other advisors.

Your Investment Policy Statement

A liquidity event will very likely change you in some manner. Whether it makes you more wary of taking risks or motivates you to focus on maximizing returns depends on you and your goals. Are you focusing on a shorter-term goal of education for children? Or

---

76   David Leonhardt, "It's Called 'a Loan,' but It's Far Sweeter," *New York Times,* February 3, 2002, https://www.nytimes.com/2002/02/03/business/it-s-called-a-loan-but-it-s-far-sweeter.html

are you building a cushion for your own retirement? If you and your financial advisor have planned for the event, you will go through it with better direction and confidence. Having an investment policy statement in place prior to the liquidity event provides the necessary guidance and direction as the proceeds arrive. Your investment policy statement details your personal financial goals and objectives, and it explains the investment strategies to be implemented based on your risk tolerance, time constraints, tax situation, and the resources needed. If you have not planned for it, then contact your advisor immediately to find the best path for you.

A liquidity event can be life changing for you and your loved ones. Be certain that funds for taxes are in a non-volatile investment such as treasury bills or bank CDs.

Takeaway

- If a private company has reinvested cash flow in the business in lieu of paying out dividends, the liquidity event will be the first time founders, investors, and employees receive a significant return on their investment.

- The most common liquidity events occur when a company goes public with an initial public offering (IPO) or is bought out by another company.

- As a company insider, you must follow a myriad of rules and regulations when you divest of your company's stock. Consulting corporate counsel and other advisors prior to liquidating shares is advised.

- A liquidity event can be life changing for you and your loved ones. Be certain you've set aside enough for taxes in a safe, nonfluctuating savings vehicle.

FOR EXECUTIVES AND UPPER MANAGEMENT

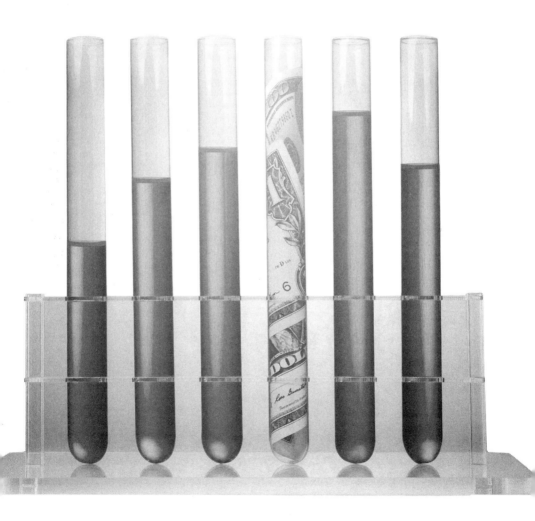

CHAPTER NINE

MAXIMIZING INCENTIVE COMPENSATION PLANS

Senior executives and upper management are compensated in many ways beyond their base salaries. Stock options, restricted stock, restricted stock units, nonqualified deferred compensation plans, qualified plans, golden parachutes, phantom stock, business expense reimbursements, and executive bonus plans are among the ways a company can reward its management team and directors. As we've discussed in previous chapters, along with the benefits of these plans, there are various caveats to be aware of. Income and estate tax consequences, lockup periods, vesting schedules, regulatory requirements, and other "golden handcuffs" are all reasons why founders and executives receiving such benefits should have a team of knowledgeable advisors and experts prepared to assist them as they navigate their careers and business decisions around these offerings.

Stock Options

At first glance, stock options sound like a great idea. The company that employs you rewards your loyalty by letting you own stock and share in the success you are contributing to with all your hard work. What could go wrong? A great deal could go wrong if you don't understand how options work.

Options allow you to buy a given number of shares of your company's stocks at a specified price within a certain period. These options vest over time, usually in tranches, such as 25 percent every year over four years. They have both a grant date (the date they're awarded to you) and an expiration date, which is often about ten years after the grant date. When you exercise them, you buy stock in the company at a set price, known as the strike price. I'm sure you can already see the advantages. A company can compensate employees without spending valuable cash up front, and later, the company can acquire contributions when the employees exercise the shares. Once the options vest, you can exercise them, gift them if the plan allows it, or retain them for future exercise. Within each of these three areas, various strategies exist to help you mitigate taxes and manage the risks.

How Does a Stock Option Work?

The following example from AllBusiness.com explains how stock options are granted and exercised:[77]

- ABC, Inc., hires employee John Smith.

- As part of his employment package, ABC grants John options to acquire forty thousand shares of ABC's common stock at twenty-five cents per share (the fair market value of a share of ABC common stock at the time of grant).

- The options are subject to a four-year vesting with one year cliff vesting, which means that John has to stay employed with ABC for one year before he gets the right to exercise ten thousand of the options and then he vests the remaining thirty thousand options at the rate of 1/36 a month over the next thirty-six months of employment.

- If John leaves ABC or is fired before the end of his first year, he doesn't get any of the options.

- After his options are "vested" (become exercisable), he has the option to buy the stock at twenty-five

---

77   Richard Harroch, "How Employee Stock Options Work in Startup Companies," allbusiness. com, https://www.allbusiness.com/how-employee-stock-options-work-in-startup-companies-103450-1.html.

- cents per share, even if the share value has gone up dramatically.

- After four years, all forty thousand of his option shares are vested if he has continued to work for ABC.

- ABC becomes successful and goes public. Its stock trades at $20 per share.

- John exercises his options and buys forty thousand shares for $10,000 (40,000 x 25 cents).

- John turns around and sells all forty thousand shares for $800,000 (40,000 x the $20 per share publicly traded price), making a nice profit of $790,000 before taxes.

Two Types of Stock Options

There are two basic types of employee stock options: nonqualified stock options (NQSOs) and incentive stock options (ISOs). The main difference between the two occurs at the exercise of the option. NQSOs incur ordinary income tax on the difference between the strike price and the fair market value of the stock on the date of exercise. With ISOs the difference between the strike price and the fair market value on the date of exercise is an Alternative Minimum Tax (AMT) preference item. This means they may or may not trigger an AMT, but if you exercise ISOs, you should notify your tax advisor before year-end, so there are no surprises. If shares obtained through exercising ISOs are held for one year or more from the exercise date, the difference between the strike price and fair market value on the date of exercise will qualify for the lower capital gains tax rates. This can be a risky proposition, though; if the share price falls, you'll still owe taxes on the difference between the exercise price and the fair market value of the stock on the date of exercise. As an example, your ISOs have an exercise price for ABC stock at $10 per share, and you exercise the option when ABC stock is selling for $50 per share for a gain of $40 per share. However, you want to pay the lower long-term capital gains rates on the $40 per share gain, so you hang onto the shares for twelve months and a day. But when you go to sell the shares the fair market price of ABC stock is $5 per share. You'll still owe long-term capital gains tax on the difference between the $10 exercise price and the $50 per share market price a year ago when you exercised the option—ouch!

Design a Plan to Exercise Your Stock Options

I'm often asked, "When is the best time to exercise my options?" We can't know for certain what the future will bring, and the stock market fluctuates for many reasons. Therefore, I would say you'll only know the best time with hindsight. So, it is best to establish a disciplined divesting strategy. We recommend our clients revisit their stock options every quarter, and consider the following criteria before they exercise:

- your financial goals and objectives, and how much the options can contribute toward them;

- the current value of the stock in relation to its historical valuation metrics like the P/E ratio, ROE, CAGR, etc.;

- your year-to-date tax situation, and the impact exercising options will have on it; and

- what other strategies can be utilized to offset the tax ramifications of exercising options, such as increasing pretax contributions to nonqualified deferred compensation plans or charitable donations to your private foundation.

Once all these factors have been considered, some or all of the vested options should be exercised each quarter. If the underlying stock is undervalued, then exercising fewer option contracts might make sense, and if the underlying stock is overvalued, then exercising a greater amount should be considered. Obviously if the strike price is greater than the underlying stock, then none of the options should be exercised because this would mean they are "underwater." Conversely, when the exercise price is less than the underlying stock, the options are considered "in the money," and that may be the best time to exercise them.

I can't emphasize enough the importance of having a systematic divesting plan. Over the years, I have seen clients insist that the stock price is going to keep climbing, and they resist my pleas to "take some chips off the table" only to see the stock price plummet, the options go underwater, and the total value of the previous in-the-money options vanish. I've seen clients sit on options with a valuation that would allow them to retire at that very moment, only to wait for more gains, and then have to wait another two years for the same valuation to materialize again. You can be rest assured they pulled the trigger that time!

So, how do you figure out your number and when to exercise options toward it? That's where a trusted advisor comes in, someone who will guide you through the wealth management process, and who has a team of experts to evaluate all aspects of your financial plans and determine the impact your stock options will have on the successful implementation of those plans. Having seen the good, the bad, and the ugly, I know how important it is to meet periodically with your advisor throughout the year. This way, you are able to evaluate which grants you have, which are vested, which are unvested, what the strike price is, and what the current value of the shares is. You and your advisor can also look at the valuation of the company itself in relation to the stock price. This type of review is crucial in determining which action—if any—to take.

How to Exercise Stock Options

If you'd like to own all the shares available through exercising your options, a cash-for-stock exercise or exercise-and-hold transaction would be appropriate. You simply purchase the stocks with your own cash at the option price and hold on to the shares. Suppose you don't have enough cash for a cash exercise. You might then consider an exercise-and-sell-to-cover transaction where you exercise the options and then sell just enough shares to cover the option cost, taxes, and brokerage fees. You then receive the net proceeds in the form of shares. If it's cash you'd like, then an exercise-and-sell transaction makes sense. In this situation, you use a company-selected brokerage firm, which advances funds to cover the exercise price, taxes, and broker fees, and immediately sell all the shares. Following the transaction, you can take the cash or use it to diversify your investments among other securities.

The Difference with Biotech Stock Options

As you've already seen in the early chapters of this book, the biotech industry changes rapidly and often unpredictably. Therefore, you need to be diligent in overseeing your stock options and working your plan accordingly.

What makes the industry exciting is also what contributes to its lack of predictability. Picture this industry of small startups and younger companies side by side with big pharma. You need to consider the stability of the company as well as the stock price in relation to its similar firms as you make decisions that will enhance or detract from your equity compensation package.

WHAT'S IN THE PIPELINE?

A biotech company's pipeline of pending products—the types of drugs and the various stages of clinical trials they are in—can also affect options exercising decisions. Knowing the prospects of what's in the pipeline (or not) can have a substantial impact on whether it's a good time to exercise your stock options.

According to the FDA definition, the pipeline starts with Phase 1, a study with twenty to one hundred healthy volunteers or people with the disease/condition.[78] The goal of the study, which can last several months, is to ascertain safety and dosage. Approximately 70 percent of drugs move to Phase 2, which is focused on efficacy and side effects. This can last as long as two years. Only about 33 percent of drugs progress to Phase 3, which can last from one to four years. Only 25 to 30 percent move on to the final phase.

As you can see, understanding where a company's products are in the pipeline—and how many they have in the pipeline—are essential tools that will help you and your advisor determine the state of your options. You also need to know which patents are expiring and whether the company has anything pending to replace them.

---

78 "Step 3: Clinical Research," US Food and Drug Administration, https://www.fda.gov/ForPatients/Approvals/Drugs/ucm405622.htm.

Restricted Stock and Restricted Stock Units

Because of their complexity and uncertainty, stock options appear to be getting replaced with restricted stock and restricted stock units (RSUs). Restricted stock shareholders can still be paid dividends and have voting rights, while RSUs do not until they vest. Similar to stock options, these incentive plans have a vesting schedule and serve as motivation for employees to continue productive employment with the company. Unlike stock options, however, they simply obtain their value as the grantee vests into them. Basically, they go from being restricted shares to common stock shares according to the vesting schedule, and, as they vest, the employee pays taxes on the value of the vested shares.

SECTION 83(B) ELECTION

Another difference between restricted stock and RSUs is that, with restricted stock, a Section 83(b) election can be made, and with RSUs, it cannot. An 83(b) election, which must be made within thirty days from the grant date, allows restricted stock recipients to recognize ordinary income on the restricted stock amount on the grant date, and pay the lower capital gains rate on any appreciation when they vest and are sold. So if the recipient believes the stock has good appreciation potential from the grant date to the vesting date, the 83(b) election allows him or her to pay more favorable capital gains rates on the appreciation rather than ordinary income tax rates that would apply without the 83(b) election. However, if an 83(b) election is made, and the recipient doesn't vest, taxes were paid for the income that was recognized when the 83(b) election was made, and no tax deduction is allowed. Also, without an 83(b) election, if the company shares are not traded publicly when they vest, ordinary income taxes will be owed on the full amount when they vest, and the recipient needs to pay the taxes on a stock they can't sell. This is why many startups prefer to grant stock options instead. However, as you'll see below, new Revenue Code Section 83(i) might solve this dilemma.

In anticipation of the vesting schedule for restricted stock or RSUs, you should have a plan to complement your goals and objectives, mitigate the tax impact, and determine if it is better to hold the shares, gift them, or divest of them immediately. Your investment policy statement and comprehensive wealth management plan can clarify, guide, and direct these decisions.

The Enron scandal exposed how company officials hid billions of dollars in debt from their board of directors and audit committee. Company stock—once as high as $90.75 per share—dropped to less than one dollar by the end of 2001, and shareholders filed a $40 billion lawsuit. Enron filed for bankruptcy, and similar companies were also exposed for breaking tax laws and issuing worthless stock. Clearly, potential employees across the board found little appeal in the stock options of the past. Companies then began issuing restricted stock units, something that had in the past been offered mainly to executives. Between 2003 and 2005, the median number of stock options granted by Fortune 1000 firms dropped from 40 percent, while the median number of restricted stock awards increased by nearly 41 percent over the same period.[79]

So how do you collect dividends with RSUs? You don't—at least not in the traditional way. The company doesn't allocate actual shares, so you can't collect dividends, but your employer may pay dividend

---

79   "Restricted Stock Unit—RSU," Investopedia, December 12, 2018, https://www.investopedia.com/terms/r/restricted-stock-unit.asp#ixzz5Vf3MX3Ne.

equivalents. Those equivalents can then be moved into an escrow account to help offset withholding taxes. They can also be reinvested should you choose to purchase additional shares. Of course, those equivalents will be taxed as gross income on the vesting date.[80]

SECTION 83(I) ELECTION

The Tax Cuts and Jobs Act of 2018 introduced a new election for startups and their employees. Code Section 83(i) will allow some shareholders the ability to defer, for up to five years, the taxation of compensation paid to employees of "eligible corporations" in the form of "qualified stock." This allows eligible private companies to issue stock options or restricted stock units to eligible employees in exchange for performance of services. The employee can elect, at time of vesting, to defer for up to five years the income taxes that otherwise would be due on the date the stock vests or is transferred to the employee. When the election is made, the holding period for long-term capital gain treatment begins the date the stock is transferred to the employee. Also, an 83(i) election can be rescinded at any time after it is made. Restricted stock can be viewed as an excellent recruiting, retention, and incentive program for employers. The eligibility rules for which corporations can issue qualified stock grants—and to whom—are very clear. It is vital you consult your corporate counsel or business attorney before promising anything to new or existing employees.

---

80   Ibid.

Nonqualified Deferred Compensation

In an established company, most employees at the executive level will have access to a nonqualified deferred compensation plan. These plans act as supplements to a 401(k). As a rule, beginning in 2019, executives will max out their 401(k) at $19,000 to $25,000 a year, depending on their age, and they need a strategy to shelter more money from taxes. Nonqualified deferred compensation plans allow these executives to put as much as they want into a pretax vehicle, similar to a 401(k). However, these plans are not protected by ERISA laws, and they are considered an asset of the company. Therefore, it is at risk to the company's creditors.

A TAX-MITIGATION TOOL

Still, if you are confident in the stability and safety of your company, this is an excellent tool to use to complement divesting or vesting of stock options and restricted shares. In anticipation of these other compensation plans vesting and coming due, you can use the deferred compensation plan to avoid double taxation. Or you can mitigate the impact of these events and soften the tax hit on your overall income.

You might use such a plan as a tool to make sure you don't stray into a higher tax bracket or eliminate other deductions and exemptions. It's a tax mitigation tool that should, again, be considered in the overall scheme of things. It is not a place to put a certain amount of money and ignore. It should be well coordinated with your entire financial plan.

A DIVERSIFICATION TOOL

Most deferred compensation plans allow you to diversify in mutual funds or mutual-fund type investments, making it a diversification tool in addition to a tax-mitigation tool.

Stock, stock options, and restricted shares are all creating a concentrated position in the same company that provides your income. Risk management and tax reduction strategies are critical because the concentrated shares can be very volatile and unpredictable. The price of the stock can be influenced by government regulations, competitors' innovations and advancements, or your own company's faltering. In the biotech industry, share price can be influenced by drug patents expiring and by FDA test results. As we discussed earlier, your human capital—where you derive your income and wealth creation from— should also influence how you invest and diversify your holdings.

Thus, the consequences of hanging onto a concentrated position can be both positive or adverse. Sometimes, you may be mandated to maintain a certain amount of your company's stock, and that is where these strategies become critical for you. Most CEOs don't like to see their own management team divesting too heavily or quickly, and it can have an impact on one's career advancement if these written, or unwritten, rules are breached.

ACCOUNTED FOR AND AUTOMATED

At our firm, our clients have all their plans online and accounted for in one place, and as the dynamics shift, we're available to consult, strategize, and keep them in compliance. Generally, we want to meet with our clients who have these compensation plans at least two to three times a year. We can then keep track of the goals and objectives these assets need to be available for. Whether it's a vacation home, yacht, or a sabbatical, we need to coordinate plans to reduce taxes and market risks, and make sure adequate assets are available to have the goals materialize. Having everything accounted for and automated allows us to be very proactive, to utilize the plans efficiently and effectively in a timely and cohesive manner. There's no second guessing. We need to adjust and adapt as circumstances change, and believe me, they will change. One of most important things we do is look at the big picture and help our clients get the clarity and insight as to how all these tools can complement each other and function together in an optimum manner.

Takeaway

- Various exercise strategies exist to help you mitigate taxes and manage risks with stock options, restricted stock, and RSUs.

- The various incentive compensation plans should be approached and utilized in a cohesive and well-thought-out plan. In and of themselves, they're great; combined, they become a powerful wealth generation and protection plan.

- The biotech drug pipeline—the stage of clinical trials and commercialization—affects the stock price and plan decision-making.

- A nonqualified deferred-compensation plan is both a tax-mitigation tool and an all-important diversification tool.

CHAPTER TEN

PREPARING
FOR EXIT

One of the first things you must plan for as you embark upon a successful career or form a startup company is when and how you are going to leave it. Nothing lasts forever, and you don't want to leave your departure to chance, especially not in an industry where situations change rapidly and often drastically. This brings us to your exit strategy. What are your time constraints, and how long before you will need the money? The more you understand the bigger picture and what you value in life, the better you can plan. What are you trying to get out of your career or startup, and why are you working so hard? What is your quality of life? Is it worth it or not? These are all the considerations we help clients weigh, and it's what you need to do as you plan your exit strategy. This is most important for entrepreneurs, as they may desire a liquidity event rather than a career and running a company. Will they become a serial entrepreneur, or will it be a one and done? Perhaps a liquidity event can launch a whole other career, such as venture capitalist or angel investor for other startups. We live in a free country based on capitalism, and the possibilities are endless.

Most people are in it for the long haul. Everyone still needs an exit strategy and a goal. That will determine how long you keep working, how long you hang onto your company's stock, and how soon you might start trying to divest of it. An important part of our job is helping people think about and address these issues that are easy to put off when you are involved in the day-to-day of a career and family.

Remember, What's the Number?

When considering retirement, the rule of thumb is you'll need to replace at least 70 to 80 percent of your current income. Another way to look at it is by outlining your needs, wants, and desires and assigning each one a dollar amount. This way you can run some "what if" scenarios around various outflows depending on what you can and might like to do. Other factors include your health and your spouse's health, your family's history of longevity, and your location. Then, you'll need to project how inflation and taxes will impact your expenses. Finally, you'll need to forecast this all out about thirty years or so, and include a reasonable rate of return on your assets throughout the projected time.

Needless to say, unless you know how to create an Excel spreadsheet that can do all this, you should work with a professional such as a Certified Financial Planner (CFP) or a CPA with the additional designation of Personal Financial Specialist (PFS). Ask the planner or specialist to use software that will provide a Monte Carlo simulation to analyze hundreds of market scenarios that could play out throughout the future. This will give you a best, worst, and average case scenario as to the viability of your retirement decision. Other stress tests, such as a bad market right out of the gate, potential long-term care expenses, or a premature death should be considered as well.

That's a good start regarding the numbers, but what will you do to occupy your time when you retire?

Define Your Retirement Lifestyle

It's never too early to think about what you'd like to do in retirement. It's good to keep busy. I've seen people who have too much time on their hands, and all they can think about is their next ailment. It's important to not only have a financial plan, but to also have a plan for the lifestyle you'd like to have in retirement.

First off, you may have commitments, such as occasionally helping with your grandchildren—I want to emphasize the word *occasionally*; I would not recommend you become the full-time day care, unless absolutely necessary. I'm sure you can imagine the time, energy, and money that go into a commitment like that.

After your obligations, consider your hobbies and interests. These are the things you love to do now but never seem to have enough time to fully enjoy. Things like sports, music, art, mentorship, volunteering, gardening, etc. The list goes on, so really try to focus on two or three things that you've always wanted to do or just love to do. Any more than this, and you may not have enough time for them all. Also, consider seasonality. If something ends in the winter, make sure you can replace it with something else for that season.

Finally, you've probably heard the phrase "health is wealth." Well, I'd have to agree with that. No matter how much money you've socked away, if you can't enjoy it, it probably wasn't worth all the time away from your family and friends while you were working to accumulate it. So, take care of your physical and mental health now and throughout your lifetime. This will pay more dividends than any portfolio in retirement. Don't get me wrong, financial health is critical to support your retirement lifestyle. Just don't sacrifice your health to achieve it. That's why it's best to understand the number that will allow you to say retirement is affordable and work is optional, and once you've achieved the number, you control the shots. You get the point: have a good work/life balance now, make sure you know what you're going to do with your time when you no longer want to work—and stay busy!

> *Financial health is critical to support your retirement lifestyle. Just don't sacrifice your health to achieve it.*

Preretirement Asset Management

If you're five to seven years from retirement, you're in what we call "the red zone." In case you're not familiar with the term, it comes from American football. It is when the opposing team is within twenty yards of crossing into the end zone. As in football, you can't afford to fumble or lose the ball—your investment portfolio—at this point. During this time, if the stock market wanders into bear territory— with prices dipping 20 percent from a previous high—and most of your money is in your company's stock, it could dramatically impact your ability to maintain your desired lifestyle in retirement. It might mean you'll have to work a little longer or adjust your spending. Either way, this is not an ideal situation. So let's see what we can do to help secure your retirement when you're in the red zone.

MANAGING CONCENTRATED STOCK POSITIONS

If you go to a cocktail party with your friends and neighbors and start whining about the complexities of managing and unwinding a multimillion-dollar concentrated stock position, you're probably not going to find too many sympathetic ears, and might find yourself all alone on the other side of the room. This is definitely not something to bemoan. In fact, it's what is known as a "Cadillac problem." It's a fortunate, yet most likely, a hard-earned position to be in. Your company stock is also likely the largest asset in your entire portfolio. That's why it is critical that you manage it effectively and are aware of the most cost-effective, tax-efficient risk management strategies available to you. Here, we'll explore the following:

- selling and divesting

- index-proxy accounts

- using stock options

- exchange funds

- stock protection funds

- tax avoidance trusts

In earlier chapters, we talked about founders, directors, and executives having concentrated positions in their company stock in the form of common stock, restricted stock, RSUs, and stock options. Using one or a combination of these strategies may be critical to keeping your wealth intact.

Sell and Divest

Sometimes the best and easiest strategy is to sell the shares outright and invest the proceeds into a well-balanced and diversified portfolio of other securities. Before doing that, you must establish the cost basis—the amount at which the shares were bought—to determine the amount of capital gain, if any. Also, the amount of time the shares have been held will determine whether the gain is a short-term or long-term capital gain. As noted earlier, short-term gains are taxed at ordinary income tax rates, and long-term gains qualify for lower capital gain tax rates. Also, shareholders who are insiders of the company, to avoid any accusations of trading on nonpublic material information, will need to disclose the proposed sales ahead of time through the use of a 10b5-1 plan. The plan must be written before the executive becomes aware of the material inside information. It must either specify the amount, price, and date, or provide a written formula for determining those parameters, such as "On the first market day of each quarter, sell two thousand shares of *XYZ* stock as long as the sales price equals or exceeds $30 per share." The executive should not have any discretion over how, when, or whether to execute the plan. Also, the executive cannot enter into or alter a corresponding or hedging position regarding the same stock. Once a plan is in place, no other transactions in the company stock should take place. Termination provisions could be in place for extraneous events such as the company's merger or acquisition, the client's divorce, or a serious illness.

Index-Proxy Account

An index-proxy account uses a separately managed account (SMA) to diversify around the concentrated holding and attempt to mimic the rate of return and risk characteristics of a stock index such as the S&P 500. An SMA is a portfolio of individual securities managed on your behalf by a professional asset management firm. In this case the asset manager will have specific instructions to not add any more shares of your particular company's stock. Other shares in the account can be harvested for capital losses to use against gains in the concentrated position, further diversifying the concentrated position in a tax-advantaged manner. This is performed through advanced portfolio optimization software programs that asset managers utilize and customize for a particular holding. Index mutual funds and ETFs simply cannot replicate the tax efficiency and portfolio optimization levels that an SMA can achieve.

Using Stock Options

If not restricted by company policy or implied rules, buying a protective put option to hedge the downside risk of your concentrated position is another possibility. This allows you to lock in a stated price over a set period that you could sell the shares at if the price of the shares decline. Or, you could just sell the put contract itself. Although this is a good and logical strategy, it can also be very expensive and not very tax efficient.

Selling covered call options with a strike price above the current market price of the stock provides additional income that can offset potential losses when the price of the stock goes down. However, the call limits your upside profit potential if the share price reaches the call's strike price. You can either buy the call back at the higher price or deliver the shares at the set price.

A third strategy, establishing a collar, involves selling call options and buying a protective put with the proceeds from the sale of the call options, potentially making it a cost-free transaction. If the stock price remains within the strike prices of the put and call, the options expire with no value: no harm, no foul. However, if the stock price goes higher than the call's strike price, you'll lose the premium you received for the call and may have to deliver the shares, but you were protected against the downside all along.

Exchange Funds

Another possibility is to trade some of your stock for shares in an exchange fund (a private placement limited partnership that pools your shares with those of other investors who also may have concentrated stock positions). After a set period, generally seven years, each of the exchange fund's shareholders is entitled to a prorated portion of the portfolio. Taxes are postponed until you sell those shares; you pay taxes on the difference between the value of the stock you contributed and the price received for your exchange fund shares. Though it provides no liquidity for seven years, an exchange fund may help minimize taxes while providing greater diversification (though diversification alone does not guarantee a profit or ensure against a loss).

Be sure to check on the costs involved with an exchange fund as well as what other securities it holds. At least 20 percent must be in non-publicly traded assets or real estate, and the more overlap between your shares and those already in the fund, the less diversification you achieve.

Stock Protection Funds

Stock protection funds are a relatively new form of insurance for con-centrated positions. These concentrated positions are with sharehold-ers who wish to keep their shares, hoping to obtain the upside appre-ciation potential and dividend income, but mitigating the downside risk of holding the shares. Unlike exchange funds, shareholders can sell their shares at any time, but the program will run for five years until it is terminated. Basically, shareholders of different companies holding concentrated positions will pay up to 5 to 10 percent of their position's value in cash into a pool of money managed very conserva-tively, generally in treasury bills. At the end of five years, each partici-pant will have a claim on the insurance pool. Any investors who've experienced losses on their positions will obtain cash to mitigate or eliminate their losses. Any excess cash left over after making investors who incurred losses whole will be shared equally by the investors whose positions appreciated. This program is relatively new, so there are few illustrations of cases where a position ceases operations or ceases to be publicly traded.

Tax Avoidance Trusts

If you want income rather than growth from your stock, you might transfer shares to a trust. If you have highly appreciated stock, consider donating it to a charitable remainder trust (CRT). You receive a tax deduction when you make the contribution. Typically, the trust can sell the stock without paying capital gains taxes and reinvest the proceeds to provide an income stream for you as the donor. When the trust is terminated, the charity retains the remaining assets. You can set a payout rate that meets both your financial objectives and your philanthropic goals; however, the donation is irrevocable. A private foundation or donor-advised fund can be the charitable beneficiary of the trust to retain some familial control for the next generation. A wealth replacement trust can be funded with life insurance; the tax savings and income stream from the CRT can cover the premiums. Also, a non-income charitable remainder trust defers income until a later date, such as retirement, when the income spigot can be turned on. Perhaps the donor will be in a lower tax bracket at that time.

Another option is a charitable lead trust (CLT), which in many ways is a mirror image of a CRT. With a typical CLT, the charity receives the income stream for a specified time; the remainder goes to your beneficiaries. There are costs associated with creating and maintaining trusts. You receive a tax deduction based on the present value of the future stream of income that will be paid to the charity. As stated above, a private foundation or donor-advised fund can be the charitable beneficiary of the trust to retain some familial control for the next generation to deliver and fulfill the charitable intent.

These are all valid tax-efficient diversification tools for concentrated positions that should be approached cautiously and with an experienced wealth management team. They should be considered and coordinated based on your goals, time horizon, tolerance for risk, and income and estate tax situation.

EMPLOYEE STOCK OPTIONS

As you saw in the last chapter, you need to plan how and when to exercise your stock options. As we discussed, your decisions about how to handle stock options depend on where the company is in its life cycle in relation to your overall wealth management plans. It also depends on where the industry is in the business cycle, and how the industry is looked upon from a regulatory standpoint. Is the current federal administration friendly toward the industry, or is there greater interest in controlling and regulating it? As with any other forms of stock concentration, the consideration of your goals, time horizon, risk tolerance, and income and estate tax situation should be evaluated before embarking on a plan to exercise your employee stock options. As mentioned before, carefully managing options with other tax-reduction strategies like simultaneously increasing contributions to nonqualified deferred compensation plans will lessen the tax hit. Coupling this with a charitable giving strategy could eliminate any tax burden. This is where the combined efforts of an experienced and knowledgeable wealth management team can be indispensable and pay for themselves many times over.

HUMAN CAPITAL

Some people should be divesting of concentrated positions more aggressively, and others should hang on to concentrated positions longer. An individual's situation may be unique, especially when it comes to human capital. We know that if your human capital is totally dependent on one company in the biotech industry, you should be investing your personal assets more conservatively and should consider divesting a concentrated position more aggressively than someone who has inherited wealth already fully diversified elsewhere. Also, if appropriate, you need to consider your spouse's or partner's human capital as well. If your spouse is an executive of a consumer staple-type company like Coca-Cola, your spouse may be vested in a defined benefit pension plan and be well-diversified and funded in a 401(k) and IRA, so you can possibly afford to maintain a concentrated stock position in a biotech startup longer and invest your funds more aggressively. The human capital component of your overall wealth management plan is critical to understanding if you should hold or divest of your concentrated position and how you should manage divestiture.

DIVERSIFICATION AND TAX MITIGATION

With concentrated positions, your goal should be diversification and tax mitigation. That is how you manage the risk of a concentrated stock position—where most if not all of your investments are connected with your current company. As always, your goals come before any strategy or "rule." A simple approach is to start not by buying more of the concentrated stock, but selling it. You can also give away the stock to your heirs or to charity.

As Tim Kochis states in *Managing Concentrated Stock Wealth: An Advisor's Guide to Building Customized Solutions*, "The real world offers very little that's certain. Investment optimization is always a guessing game about what the future may hold. Some guesses are more logically sound and better informed than others, but perfection is not in the cards. Partial solutions are far better than none. Combinations of solutions are often quite appropriate. But ultimately—especially because there can be no certainty—the simplest, fastest, least costly solutions are very often the best."[81]

---

81   Tim Kochis, *Managing Concentrated Stock Wealth: An Advisor's Guide to Building Customized Solutions* (Hoboken, New Jersey: John Wiley & Sons, 2016).

Asset Allocation and Modern Portfolio Theory

As you begin to divest your concentrated stock position (CSP), and as you accumulate wealth separate from your CSP for that matter, you should have an investment discipline and philosophy that can navigate through any type of market condition, good or bad. What we find works well, and what we have adhered to for the past thirty years, is the discipline of asset allocation and modern portfolio theory. Asset allocation is the process of diversifying your assets across different types of investments, such as stocks, bonds, real estate, and cash.

Modern portfolio theory (MPT) looks at how these different investments, or asset classes, correlate together over time. It then determines mathematical coefficients as to the patterns that exist between these asset classes. Based on this information, the theory is that for any given level of risk an investor is willing to assume, there is an efficient mix of these assets that can be built to obtain the maximum rate of return for the assumed level of risk. Hence, this is called the *Efficient Frontier*. Any portfolio that intersects, or lies on, the Efficient Frontier is deemed to be efficient and should obtain the maximum level of return for that level of risk. An inefficient portfolio is one that assumes a higher level of risk than needed to assume a certain rate of return. A concentrated stock position in one company can easily create an inefficient portfolio.

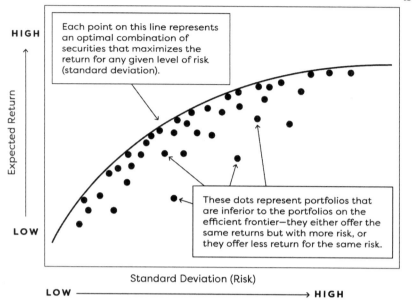

HIGH

Each point on this line represents an optimal combination of securities that maximizes the return for any given level of risk (standard deviation).

Expected Return

These dots represent portfolios that are inferior to the portfolios on the efficient frontier—they either offer the same returns but with more risk, or they offer less return for the same risk.

LOW

Standard Deviation (Risk)

LOW ———————————→ HIGH

POSTMODERN PORTFOLIO THEORY

Various critics have challenged MPT for a couple of reasons. First, during the 2000–2001 and 2008–2009 periods, most investments declined in value together, creating a coefficient of one, meaning no diversification. Second, MPT relies on the standard deviation of an investment's performance, which can penalize a fund for obtaining larger upside returns than its benchmark or peer group. Because most investors don't mind getting larger upside returns and are more concerned with the downside risk of an investment, proponents of postmodern portfolio theory (PMPT) are beginning to have their voices heard. PMPT uses the Sortino ratio as opposed to the standard deviation to judge investments on their merit. Named after Frank A. Sortino, professor emeritus in finance at San Francisco State

---

82   Investing Answers, "Efficient Frontier," accessed January 2019, investinganswers.com/financial-dictionary/investing/efficient-frontier-1010.

University, the Sortino ratio differentiates harmful volatility from total overall volatility by focusing on an asset's standard deviation of negative returns. Much of our research in choosing individual holdings for our portfolios today includes evaluating an investment's Sortino ratio.

Takeaway

- To embark upon a successful exit, you must "know your number."

- Understanding your human capital component in the context of your overall wealth management plan is critical to implementing a practical divesting and reinvestment strategy.

- Diversification and tax mitigation are essential to managing the risk of concentrated stock.

- The discipline of asset allocation and the philosophy of modern portfolio theory will help you navigate through any type of market condition.

- Postmodern portfolio theory uses the Sortino ratio instead of the standard deviation to judge the merit of investments.

CHAPTER ELEVEN

POSTRETIREMENT ASSET DISTRIBUTION

Managing your money in retirement is different from managing it while you are working. While you are working and accumulating assets, fluctuations and drawdowns in the market work to your favor: you're able to buy shares cheaper. In retirement, drawdowns and pullbacks in the market can be devastating to your investments and can decrease how much income you can sustainably take out of them over your lifetime. You have both fixed and variable sources of income and expenses in retirement, and you need to understand what and how much they are, and whether inflation will affect them. Your fixed income sources may include Social Security, a defined-benefit pension plan, distributions from nonqualified deferred compensation plans, an annuity, and even income from a board seat or consulting work. These income sources are usually highly predictable, and some may come with an annual cost-of-living increase. Typically you will decide when to begin to taking them, how much you'll take out each year, whether you'll provide your survivor income if you predecease the term of the payout, and possibly how long the distributions can continue. These decisions can mean the difference between receiving hundreds of thousands of dollars more over your and your survivors' lives, or not.

Social Security

A whole chapter could be devoted solely to this topic and not scratch the surface. In fact, we provide our clients with a booklet, updated every year, that covers all the specifics of Social Security, Medicare, and Medicaid. If you are reading this book, it's likely Social Security will represent less than one-third of your post-retirement income. This means you will have done well enough on your own by accumulating significant assets in company stock, retirement plans, and other accounts to eliminate or at least marginalize your need for Social Security. However, since you've paid into the system your entire working life, you might as well reap whatever benefits you're entitled to and try to maximize them for you and your family.

Having been in this business for more than thirty years, I can see the trend of people waiting longer to take benefits. However, you first become eligible to take an early retirement benefit at age sixty-two, and you'll receive approximately 70 percent of your full retirement age benefit. If married, your spouse can start taking benefits at age sixty-two as well. They will be able to take half of your benefits or their own, whichever are higher. If you wait until your full retirement age to begin receiving benefits, you'll receive 100 percent, and if you wait until age seventy, your full retirement age benefit will increase 8 percent per year until then. You must begin payments at age seventy.

There are many other factors to consider, and if you or your spouse are entitled to a government pension, a whole other set of circumstances can arise. To me, this is not only a financial decision, but a very personal one as well. I believe it depends on your age when you retire, the significance of your investments and what type of accounts they're in, your lifestyle and spending habits, your income tax bracket, your health, and your family history of longevity. All these factors should be weighed and accounted for, and analysis should be done so you can see the potential amounts you may receive over your and your spouse's lifetimes. You need to consider various scenarios regarding what age to start receiving benefits, cost-of-living adjustments, and survivor benefits. As you'll see, your decision to start collecting Social Security benefits can also impact how you'll take distributions from IRAs and whether you should perform Roth IRA conversions. Again, this can have an impact of hundreds of thousands to potentially millions of dollars to you and your heirs.

We provide this analysis to all our wealth management clients before they make this decision.

Defined Benefit Pension Plan

By definition, a *defined-benefit plan* is an employer-sponsored retirement plan that computes employee benefits using a formula that considers several factors, such as length of employment and salary history. The company administers portfolio management and investment risk for the plan.

The plan document specifies when you are eligible to begin taking distributions from your defined benefit plan. Most often, at age sixty-five, you are eligible to receive the maximum available benefits. An actuarial calculation is made, and depending on your age, years of service, and salary history, an annual dollar amount will be determined that you can receive as income for the rest of your life. You'll also be able to take the benefit at an earlier age, but doing so will reduce the amount of that benefit. You may need to consider survivorship choices for your beneficiary as well. Again, if you choose a survivorship benefit (meaning when you die, your beneficiary will continue to receive an income for the remainder of their life), you will receive a further reduction in your own benefit. Once you make your decision, the company will buy an annuity from an insurance company to provide you the guaranteed income of your choosing. Instead of taking the lifetime income option, sometimes you'll have a choice to take a lump-sum benefit. This amount is determined by taking the present value of a future income over your life expectancy and allowing you to perform a direct rollover into your IRA. This is a nontaxable event, the proceeds can grow tax-deferred, and you will pay ordinary income tax rates when you take distributions. But unlike the lifetime income options that terminate upon your or your beneficiaries' death, the IRA could transfer to your heirs. We'll discuss taking distributions from IRAs later in this chapter.

Nonqualified Deferred Compensation (NQDC) Plans

Just as the name implies, these plans hold ordinary deferred compensation, such as salaries and bonuses, that were voluntarily deferred into the plan while you were working, or were paid in by your employer. Most plans allow you to elect how and when you can take the withdrawals at the time you elect to defer the income. The timing of withdrawals involves important tax considerations that require advance planning. Once these elections are made, there are complex rules if you want to change them. Under IRC §409A, payment events are limited to:[83]

- separation from service (as defined by the plan)

- death

- disability

- a specified time or according to a fixed schedule

- an unforeseeable emergency

- a change in the ownership or effective control of the corporation, or a change in the ownership of a substantial portion of the assets of the corporation (as defined by the plan).

---

83   "Distributions from Nonqualified Deferred Compensation Plans," Retirement Learning Center, July 11, 2018, https://retirementlc.com/distributions-from-nonqualified-deferred-compensation-plans/. For more information, see Treasury Regulation 1.409A-3: https://www.govinfo.gov/content/pkg/CFR-2013-title26-vol5/pdf/CFR-2013-title26-vol5-sec1-409A-3.pdf.

As mentioned in earlier chapters, NQDC plans are an excellent tax mitigation and investment diversification tool, but they need to be carefully integrated into an overall retirement and wealth management plan. When to defer, what type of compensation, and when to distribute decisions should take into consideration other compensation plans' vesting and exercise schedules, your future income tax situation, and your overall goals for the use of the money.

If timed properly, NQDC distributions can be excellent for the early retirement years. Before making elections to defer income into a NQDC plan, you need to understand what "timing rules" your payroll department is using in paying any FICA taxes on these deferral amounts. You don't want your distributions subject to 100 percent of the FICA tax withholdings when you receive them. It's likely that when you're deferring the income you've already paid 6.2 percent FICA on the first $128,400 of income (for 2018 wages).

In addition to tax planning, you'll need to make investment decisions in your NQDC plan. This is where we refer to your investment policy statement. Remember, your IPS will be a tool to direct and guide your overall investment decisions in a uniform and cohesive manner, all the while taking into consideration your 10b5-1 and Section 144 plans. Presumably, as you near your exit, you'll want to shift your portfolio in a more conservative direction as you'll begin taking distributions soon.

Annuities

Earlier we talked about private placement variable annuities and their benefits for ultrahigh-net-worth clients. Here we're going to talk about retail annuities for generating income in retirement. These annuities can be classified into two categories: immediate and deferred. Both types are issued by an insurance company, but have very different qualities. With an immediate annuity, you pay a lump-sum premium up front, and the insurer contracts with you to pay a certain income over a specified period, or over your lifetime. Sound familiar? It should. It is basically what a defined benefit pension plan does when you take the lifetime income payouts. The pension provider buys an immediate annuity from an insurer based on the specifics you've requested. This is called annuitizing your money An immediate annuity gives you steady, predictable income, guaranteed by the strength of the insurer. Many white papers have been written about the benefits of annuitization; however, I'm not convinced of its value. If you and your survivor die before the annuitization period is over, you may forfeit the remaining balance of your annuity to the insurance company. Basically you're betting that you will outlive your projected life expectancy.

Enter deferred annuities. A deferred annuity comes in two flavors, fixed and variable. With a deferred annuity, you put in a lump sum, it grows tax deferred, and you can plan on accessing your money later on. Fixed annuities have two types. One is like a certificate of deposit at a bank. It guarantees a fixed rate of return for a fixed amount of time. The other fixed annuity is an equity indexed fixed annuity. This type ties your rate of return to the performance of a stock index like the S&P 500. You obtain the rate of return that the index experiences over a certain period, generally with no downside risk, although the upside return will usually be capped up to a certain ceiling. A variable annuity will be invested in mutual fund-type investments called subaccounts, and will fluctuate in value like a fund. All three of these annuities can be annuitized to generate a guaranteed stream of income, or they can just be withdrawn periodically from, subject to certain surrender charges and taxes. You can also add guaranteed income benefit riders to these annuity contracts that allow you to take a certain percentage out, guaranteed for the rest of your life, without having to annuitize your money. If preserving principal and income is your main concern, these can be a good alternative to an immediate annuity, as your heirs may inherit the remaining balance if you die early on in the withdrawal phase. On the other hand, the financial services industry continues to innovate investment products, and now you can have the option of hedged and buffered investment strategies that come in the form of low-cost, daily liquid, mutual funds, and exchange-traded funds (ETFs). Also, a bond-ladder may give you as good of an income stream without the costs of an annuity. We'll talk about these coming up.

BOARD SEATS, CONSULTING, AND PART-TIME WORK

Having performed at a very high level and pace for many years, many founders and executives of companies won't want to go quietly off into the sunset. This is especially true if they still have a sizable and vested interest in seeing a large equity position continue to do well. If one can still influence the direction of the company in a positive way, it can benefit the existing management team and shareholders for these seasoned executives to continue on the board. This can be a fairly lucrative position that provides a steady income stream during "retirement."

I've seen many executives retire, only to be called back in a consulting role. Their knowledge and expertise cannot easily be replicated by a recent MBA grad, and the company can keep them on without the burden of providing benefits. In return, as a consultant, they can dictate a more flexible work schedule for themselves, derive a steady paycheck, and keep involved and active.

You may want to pursue another direction at this point in your life, however. Maybe there's a hobby you've enjoyed and can now turn into a profitable venture. Or perhaps there's something you love doing that you can now turn into a part-time job without the stress of a decision-making role. These too can help to occupy your time, create a steady stream of income, and make retirement a more fulfilling time in your life.

So, to recap: Social Security, defined benefit pension plans, non-qualified deferred compensation plans, annuities, and earned income can all create a high level of steady and predictable income in retirement. However, that doesn't mean these should be the first areas to take income from.

Investing for Income

BONDS

When we think of income investing, the first type of investment that comes to mind is bonds. When you buy a bond, you're basically lending your money to the entity that issued the bond, and the borrower promises to pay you back over a certain amount of time at a set interest rate. For example, Biogen could issue a bond that has a maturity date of November 30, 2028, with a coupon rate of 5 percent. Bought in 2018, that would be a ten-year bond paying 5 percent. Bonds can be invested in by buying a bond mutual fund, a bond ETF, or individual bonds. The value of a bond is indirectly affected by the direction interest rates are trending. Today, with interest rates on the rise, bond values have been going down. Bond mutual funds that invest in intermediate and long-term bonds are being affected the most. This is because these funds hold bonds that were issued at lower rates than the new ones that are being issued today. This makes their existing holdings less valuable—because why would anyone want a 4 percent bond when they can get a new one at 5 percent?

Some actively managed mutual funds use futures contracts to "short" interest rates, which helps their principal maintain its value better in a rising interest rate environment. These are working well today. Also, we like assembling a "bond-ladder," which works well in most rate environments. This means we take a lump sum of money and divide it up evenly over fifteen to twenty different bonds, each with a maturity date one year later than the other, hence the "ladder" analogy. Then, each year as a bond matures, we buy another bond fifteen or twenty years from maturity. As long as you hold a bond until its maturity date, you will receive your principal and interest back, provided the issuer doesn't default in the meantime. This is why we tend to stick with higher-quality companies and municipalities. We now have access to exchange traded funds that each hold several different issuers' bonds with the same, or close to the same, maturity dates. Using these funds we can create a ladder of these ETFs that now mitigates the default risk from owning one bond per entity.

STOCKS

Similar to bonds, we invest in stocks by acquiring them through stock mutual funds, stock ETFs, and individual stocks. As mentioned in the last chapter, we also obtain stocks through separately managed accounts (SMAs). There are many different types of stocks that pay generous dividends to provide income for our clients; these are generally considered value stocks. However, we don't tend to over-emphasize these. We prefer to construct portfolios weighted more closely to an index proxy, with a full diversification of growth stocks and value stocks. Utilities, real estate investment trusts (REITs), consumer staples, preferred stocks, banks, and energy stocks have all historically paid above average dividends, but over the past several years have lacked the dynamic growth potential that information technology and the life sciences have seen. In addition to that growth, with the IT and biotechnology industries having matured, we see companies like Microsoft, Amgen, and Abbvie paying and growing their dividends over time with yields as high as traditional value stocks.

ALTERNATIVES

Up until about eight years ago, most alternative investment strategies were only accessible through hedge funds, which catered to institutional and accredited investors only. These funds charge 2 percent annual management fees and take 20 percent of the gains over a certain percentage point, usually 5 percent. In addition, they have limited liquidity through quarterly tender offers that cap the amount of shares to liquidate at no more than 5 percent of the outstanding shares, with discretion to not tender anything. On top of that, there can be little transparency as to what the fund managers are buying and selling.

However, given today's technological advancements and economies of scale, we can obtain the same alternative strategies through daily liquid, low-cost mutual funds, and ETFs. These strategies include hedged equity, market neutral, long/short, private equity, and covered call writing, to name a few, and they can be used as alternatives to stock and bond allocations within a diversified portfolio to mitigate market risk and try to obtain a more consistent overall rate of return. These types of funds should help portfolios avoid steep losses when stock markets correct. The only problem is many of them haven't been around long enough to have seen an extended bear market to prove their worth. As of this writing, we saw the stock market fall 9 percent, quickly rebound the first weeks of November 2018, then dip again in December 2018. Basically, volatility has entered the stock market in a way we haven't seen in almost a decade. Perhaps these strategies will have their chance to shine. I know we have been tactically starting to utilize them more for our clients' portfolios.

TOTAL RETURN PORTFOLIOS

In the past thirty-plus years that I've been advising clients and managing their portfolios, the best strategy I've employed is a total return portfolio approach. This means we construct well-balanced, diversified portfolios of stocks, bonds, alternatives, and cash. We have portfolios ranging from conservative to aggressive—designed both for tax-qualified accounts like IRAs and retirement plans—and for nonqualified accounts, like jointly owned and trust accounts. Generally, when clients are in the distribution phase, in retirement, we will adopt a more conservative approach. But this depends strictly on the client's risk tolerance level. If they prefer more stocks and can handle the volatility, then the portfolio will accommodate their wishes. Regardless of the level of risk one assumes, we'll establish the portfolio to maintain a consistent stream of income to meet the clients' needs. Distributions go out from our custodian, TD Ameritrade, on a regular basis at the time of the month the client has indicated. Taxes are withheld, and funds are electronically transferred into their checking account for them to use, just as when they were working.

We consistently rebalance portfolios on a quarterly basis, or more often if market conditions warrant it. This means we start out with a certain target mix of assets, and as market conditions ebb and flow, we'll revisit the portfolios in light of their target mix and rebalance them back to that mix if needed. This discipline, called asset allocation and modern portfolio theory, inherently allows us to sell stocks when they are overweighted and buy them when they are underweighted. Although this doesn't protect us from losses, it gives us a good chance of minimizing losses in relation to the market, and may allow us to capture gains and obtain better pricing when markets go down.

THE FOUR PERCENT RULE

We use the following distribution rule as a guideline for our clients' income portfolios. Thankfully, in the past thirty years, which includes two of the nastiest bear markets of our lives, I've not had one client run out of money.

Some advise following the 4 percent rule to determine a portfolio's withdrawal rate. In the past, 5 percent was considered a safe amount to withdraw each year. Then, in 1994, financial advisor William Bengen conducted a study of historical returns and focused on the market downturns of the 1930s and early 1970s. Even during untenable markets, he concluded, no historical case existed in which a 4 percent annual withdrawal exhausted a retirement portfolio in fewer than thirty-three years.[84]

---

84 "Four Percent Rule," Investopedia, updated January 26, 2018, https://www.investopedia.com/terms/f/four-percent-rule.asp#ixzz5VkxQqQh1.

Yet, the correct withdrawal rate is not a simple equation. It depends on numerous factors. While some retirees who adhere to the 4 percent rule keep their withdrawal rate constant, the rule allows retirees to increase the rate to keep pace with inflation. Possible ways to adjust for inflation include setting a flat annual increase of 2 percent per year, which is the Federal Reserve's target inflation rate, or adjusting withdrawals based on actual inflation rates.

As Investopedia points out:[85]

> There are several scenarios where the 4 percent rule might not work for a retiree. A person whose portfolio features higher-risk investments than typical index funds and bonds needs to be more conservative when withdrawing money, particularly during the early years of retirement. A severe or protracted market downturn can erode the value of a high-risk investment vehicle much faster than it can a typical retirement portfolio.
>
> Further, the 4 percent rule does not work unless a retiree sticks to it year in and year out. Violating the rule one year to splurge on a major purchase can have severe consequences down the road, as this reduces the principal, which directly impacts the compound interest that the retiree depends on for sustainability.

Estate Planning

At some point, your goals may change from preserving your own wealth to passing it along to your heirs.

---

85   Ibid.

Russ Alan Prince and John J. Bowen, Jr., authors of *Becoming Seriously Wealthy: How to Harness the Strategies of the Super Rich and Ultra-Wealthy Business Owners,* put it this way:[86]

> High-quality estate planning aims both to allow you to pass on your assets as you see fit, and to minimize the state and federal tax bite that often accompanies the transfer of significant wealth to others. It's important to remember both of these goals when thinking about planning for your estate. Too often, the focus gets put entirely on how to cut the estate tax bill by as much as possible. But often, the strategies and products that enable maximum tax benefits come with strings attached that require you to entirely cede control of the assets you want to transfer—an outcome that may be highly undesirable.

I concur that the true goal of estate planning is to transfer your wealth the way you want it transferred. I also believe that until you have an updated estate plan you do not have a complete financial plan. Prince and Bowen found that more than 60 percent of successful business owners reported that they are wealthier since they created their estate plans, and more than 70 percent said that they have experienced life-changing events that could have major impacts on planning for the future since they created their original estate plans.[87]

It is recommended you review your estate plans at least every five years. Marriage, divorce, grandchildren, death, disability, and windfalls all happen and need to be considered and accounted for. The last thing you need is having your estate tied up in probate or lost to an unscrupulous heir unnecessarily.

---

86 Prince and Bowen, op. cit.: 85.
87 Prince and Bowen, op. cit.: 87.

Through the five-step comprehensive wealth management process, you can be rest assured your cash flow needs, investments, insurance plans, taxes, retirement plans, and estate plan will all be reviewed and updated, and the most tax-efficient, cost-effective, state-of-the-art, and contemporary strategies will be brought forth to help you make well-informed, educated decisions. This will not only benefit you and your loved ones today, but will have a tremendous impact for generations to come.

Takeaway

- Just as you will have fixed and variable expenses in retirement, you will also have fixed and variable sources of retirement income.

- Generally, an income distribution (retirement) portfolio will be more conservative than when you were accumulating wealth.

- A total return approach with a well-balanced, diversified portfolio and active rebalancing will reduce volatility.

- Alternative strategies are now available in liquid, cost-effective mutual funds and ETFs.

- The five-step comprehensive wealth management process will address cash flow needs, investments, insurance, taxes, retirement plans, and your estate plan.

SUMMARY

BRINGING IT ALL TOGETHER

Choosing a Wealth Manager

By now I hope I've conveyed the importance and benefit of working with a competent wealth manager. So, what is the best way to find one? As you may have guessed, there is no one, uniform standard of practice in the wealth management industry, but there are seven important aspects you need to examine.

1.   *Experience.* How many years has he or she been working as a bona fide wealth manager? How many clients do they have with situations similar to yours? Have they worked through good and bad economic and investment market cycles? What did they do to help their clients through adverse market conditions?

2.   *Credentials.* This is where you'll run into the "alphabet soup" of our industry. Although there are many certifications for financial professionals, the CFP or Certified Financial Planner designation is the most widely recognized for providing a standard of fiduciary care. Overseen by the CFP board, CFP registrants must pass a rigorous exam to acquire the designation. They then must adhere to the board's code of ethics, and obtain thirty hours of continuing education every two years to maintain their good standing and use of the certification. Other credentials of note include the Chartered Financial Consultant (ChFC), Accredited Investment Fiduciary (AIF), and the Personal Finance Specialist (PFS), which is for CPAs who wish to broaden their service offerings.

3.   *Disciplinary history.* BrokerCheck is a source for any disciplinary action that has been taken against the individual or firm you are considering working with.

Registered representatives of broker/dealers, the broker/dealers or firms themselves, and registered investment advisors, if properly registered, will show up here. Any disciplinary actions will be identified as disclosures. If there are no disclosures, then no disciplinary action has occurred. www.brokercheck.finra.org.

4. *Services offered.* How comprehensive are the firm's services? Are they focused only on investments, or will they consider all facets of your financial situation? Do they perform comprehensive wealth management or just use the phrase for advertising purposes?

5. *Process.* Does the individual or firm adhere to a well-defined and clear process to deliver the services promised? Are the services offered in writing and signed off on? Do you understand what each member of the service team does and to whom you should turn when necessary? Are you clear on the expected outcome? Are your expectations taken into consideration, and do they know what is required for you to consider the process a success in one, three, five, ten years, and beyond?

6. *Access to third-party professionals.* Will the individual have access to and collaborate with other professionals such as business attorneys, investment bankers, CPAs, estate planning attorneys, and insurance specialists? Are his or her recommendations part of the wealth management process, and are they included in the wealth manager's fees?

7. *Compensation.* How is the wealth manager compensated? Some may work on a percentage of assets under management, usually about .50 to 1.50 percent, depending

on the size of the portfolio. Others may be fee only, which should be a prearranged flat fee, not tied to assets under management. Still others may charge a commission or a combination of fees and commissions. Fees are more transparent than commissions and can allow you to judge for yourself whether the services delivered are worth the value of the fee being charged.